MW01100729

The
Hidden Majority

*A guidebook on alcohol and
other drug issues for counsellors
who work with women*

Centre
for Addiction and
Mental Health
Centre de
toxicomanie et
de santé mentale

A Pan American Health Organization / World Health Organization Collaborating Centre

))))) *canada's drug strategy*

Linda Hurtubise

Canadian Cataloguing in Publication Data
Main entry under title:

The hidden majority:
a guidebook on alcohol and other drug issues for counsellors who work with women

Includes bibliographical references.
ISBN 0-88868-256-5

1. Women – Alcohol use. 2. Women – Drug use.
3. Alcoholism counseling. 4. Drug abuse counseling.
5. Women – Counseling of. I. Ontario. Addiction Research Foundation.

HV4999.W64H53 1996   362.29'082   C96-930399-8

Disponible en français.

Printed in Canada

For information on other Centre for Addiction and Mental Health resource materials or to place an order, please contact:

Marketing and Sales Services
Centre for Addiction and Mental Health
33 Russell Street
Toronto, ON M5S 2S1
Canada

Tel.: 1-800-661-1111 or 416-595-6059 in Toronto
E-mail: marketing@camh.net

Web site: www.camh.net

Project Team

Margaret Canale   Project Coordinator, Researcher, and Writer
Addiction Research Foundation, Toronto, Ontario

Manuella Adrian   Addiction Research Foundation, Toronto, Ontario
Pearl Bader   Addiction Research Foundation, Toronto, Ontario
Julia Greenbaum   Addiction Research Foundation, Toronto, Ontario
Kristine Hollenberg   Addiction Research Foundation, London, Ontario
Eva Ingber   Addiction Research Foundation, Toronto, Ontario
Meral Kesebi   Addiction Research Foundation, Toronto, Ontario
Kathy Kilburn   Addiction Research Foundation, North Bay, Ontario
Lise Nolet   Addiction Research Foundation, Toronto, Ontario
Wendy Reynolds   Action on Women's Addictions — Research and
Education (AWARE), Kingston, Ontario
Susan Roxborough   Addiction Research Foundation, Toronto, Ontario
Cindy Smythe   Addiction Research Foundation, London, Ontario
Jackolyn Thomas   Harambee Centres Canada, Toronto, Ontario
Gwenne Woodward   Credit Valley Hospital, Mississauga, Ontario

Virginia Carver   Project Leader
Addiction Research Foundation, Ottawa, Ontario

Susan Harrison   Project Leader
Addiction Research Foundation, East Region, Ontario

This guidebook was partially funded by a contribution from the Community
Support Program of Canada's Drug Strategy, Health Canada. We thank them
for their support in recognizing the importance of and need for a resource
about women and substance use. The views expressed in the guidebook
are those of the project team and do not necessarily represent the views of
Health Canada.

Acknowledgements

The project team would like to thank the many individuals who have contributed to the development of this guidebook. We appreciate the time and thoughtfulness they gave in reviewing and commenting on this resource. The project team also thanks Kim Bell for her administrative assistance in developing resource lists related to the guidebook.

Guidebook Reviewers

Beverley Abbott	Alberta Alcohol and Drug Abuse Commission, Edmonton, Alberta
Janet Amos	Family Services of Greater Vancouver, New Westminster, British Columbia
Denise Annett	Health Canada, Ottawa, Ontario
Christine Bois	Addiction Research Foundation, East Region, Ontario
Madeline Boscoe	Women's Health Clinic, Winnipeg, Manitoba
Lorraine Chapman	Hamilton Women's Detox, Hamilton, Ontario
Michael DeVillaer	Addiction Research Foundation, Hamilton, Ontario
Sandi Harmer	Amethyst Women's Addiction Centre, Ottawa, Ontario
Marilyn Harry	Northwest Territories Status of Women Council & Northern Addiction Services, Yellowknife, Northwest Territories
Pearl Isaac	Addiction Research Foundation, Toronto, Ontario
Bonnie Johnson	Planned Parenthood Federation of Canada, Ottawa, Ontario
Meldon Kahan	Addiction Research Foundation, Toronto, Ontario
Stephen Kennedy	Addiction Assessment Services of Ottawa-Carleton, Ottawa, Ontario
Cathy Mattern	Women's Health Bureau, Health Canada, Ottawa, Ontario
Sheri McConnell	Saskatoon Mental Health Clinic and Gay & Lesbian Health Services, Saskatoon, Saskatchewan
Louise Nadeau	Université de Montréal, Outremont, Québec
Nancy Poole	British Columbia Ministry of Health, Victoria, British Columbia
Robin Room	Addiction Research Foundation, Toronto, Ontario
Helen Ross	Addiction Research Foundation, Toronto, Ontario
Wayne Skinner	Addiction Research Foundation, Toronto, Ontario
Larry Sobol	Addiction Research Foundation, Pembroke, Ontario
Trudy Watts	Pictou County Women's Centre and Tatamagouche Adult Education Centre, Scotsburn, Nova Scotia

Contents

4. Screening, Identification, Assessment, Referral

5. Women and Wellness

6. Facts about Alcohol and Other Drugs

If You Want More Information

About the Guidebook

Women's use of alcohol and other drugs occurs within the social context of how women are socialized and women's status within Canadian society. This context affects why women use drugs, the type and amount of drugs women use, and how and why women develop problems with substances. It also affects the strengths women can build on to avoid or address problems, whether women decide to seek help for their problem use, the barriers women face when they try to get help, and how successful they are in working on their substance use problems.

Much of what we know about alcohol and other drug use and how to work with people who develop problems has been based on the experiences of men. This knowledge has also then been applied to women — without recognizing that women are different. This guidebook is intended to acknowledge and address these differences. It provides information that will help counsellors better understand the context of women's substance use and intervene effectively on issues related to women's use.

What Is the Guidebook about?

This guidebook looks at alcohol and other drug use issues from the perspective of women's lives. The guidebook addresses topics such as:
- substances and how they affect women
- how to identify when alcohol or other drug use is a problem
- guidelines for appropriate use of alcohol and other legal drugs
- how to intervene and make appropriate referrals

- suggesting alternatives
- enhancing women's health

Who Is the Guidebook for?

You will find this guidebook helpful if you provide services and support directly to women. The material will be useful for health and social service providers, such as counsellors, social workers, shelter workers, psychologists, nurses, physicians, pharmacists, and other therapists. You may also find it useful if you work in the substance use field.

About the Language Used in the Guidebook

We have tried to use language that includes and embraces all women.

Language is continually changing. We have attempted to be consistent and use the most current word or phrase to represent the meaning we are trying to convey. To ensure that everyone understands the meaning of particular words, we have included the following glossary of terms to explain certain words or phrases that appear throughout the guidebook.

Alcohol-related birth effects refer to characteristics found in children as a result of the mother's use of alcohol during pregnancy. Other terms used to describe these effects include Fetal Alcohol Syndrome (FAS) and Fetal Alcohol Effects (FAE).

Continuing care generally refers to the help that a woman receives from a counsellor after she has completed a treatment program or some other form of counselling program. Other terms used to describe this type of care include "aftercare" and "follow-up."

Counsellor refers to anyone working in the helping professions. This includes all health and social service providers such as counsellors, social workers, shelter workers, psychologists, nurses, physicians, pharmacists and other therapists.

Violence refers to any form of physical or sexual abuse or assault.

Women's
Substance Use

"Women's reality is much different from men's reality. We must truly appreciate the fabric woven from the various threads in women's lives." [Harrison, 1993]

POSITIVE AND NEGATIVE ASPECTS OF WOMEN'S SOCIALIZATION

Most Canadian women are increasingly aware of the social forces that shape their lives. They recognize the negative aspects to their socialization — fewer choices than men, lack of power and control over their lives, how their worth as a person is defined, and how that may affect their self-esteem. But they also recognize the positive aspects to the roles set out for women — the development of qualities that are sources of women's overall well-being and contribute to their inner strength. Both the positive and negative aspects of women's socialization are described in the table on the following page.

When it comes to alcohol and other drugs, the negative aspects of women's socialization may result in women:
- smoking or taking diet pills to keep their weight down
- experiencing mood (e.g., depression) or anxiety disorders to such an extent that these are the primary mental health problems reported by women and/or diagnosed in women by doctors

NEGATIVE ASPECTS	POSITIVE ASPECTS
Women as People-Pleasers — Women are taught to: • seek and win the approval of others • please others instead of themselves • nurture others, conform and adapt at the expense of their own happiness, self-interest, and independence	**Women as Sensitive People** — Women tend to be skilled at: • being empathetic • cooperating with others • sharing with others • showing concern for others • taking care of others
Women as Care Givers — Women are expected to: • take care of everyone else's needs and to put other people's needs ahead of their own • place less emphasis on taking care of themselves (through health-related activities, hobbies, interests, etc.)	**Women as a Support Network** — Women are known for: • being active in their communities • developing a social support system among themselves (e.g., providing guidance and emotional support, exchanging duties such as child care) • being responsive to social policy issues that emphasize the common good
Women as Objects — Women are encouraged to: • be passive • defer to the opinions of others • pursue outward, physical beauty rather than inner, personal growth	**Women as Activists** — Women tend to become good at: • articulating their feelings • deriving strength from other women (role models) who have pushed the boundaries of the roles set out for them • being educators
Women as Unequals — Women are required to: • put up with inequality in the home, the workplace, and all aspects of Canadian society • have less say (fewer choices) about how they live their lives • deal with negative societal attitudes and stereotypes about women • cope with threats to their personal safety	**Women as Advocates** — Women use their communication and advocacy skills in: • representing the family outside the home (e.g., dealing with professionals such as doctors and children's teachers) • negotiating relationships among family members and with friends • working to create a more equitable, just, and caring society
Women as Over-Burdened Workers — Women are expected to: • be the primary caregiver for children and parents • do most of the household chores even if women decide to work outside the home out of choice and/or out of necessity	**Women as Efficient Workers** — Women develop competency in: • managing multiple role/work responsibilities • accomplishing a variety of tasks each day and performing some of them "on demand" (e.g., caring for young children)

- using alcohol and other drugs to cope with situations over which they feel they have no control
- finding it difficult to attend treatment programs due to child care and other responsibilities (e.g., not being able to get paid time off work)

For those women who experience problems with alcohol or other drug use, the positive aspects of women's socialization may result in women:
- being more successful at reducing or eliminating their alcohol and/or other drug use on their own (e.g., through self-help materials)
- sharing experiences, being sensitive, and providing support to one another in group treatment settings

Women's socialization is central to all aspects of women's lives. It sets the tone for women's lives and may result in women using negative coping strategies to deal with problems or unpleasant situations. The connections between the context of women's lives and women's reliance on alcohol or other drugs are explored throughout the guidebook.

SUBSTANCES AND THEIR EFFECTS ON WOMEN

Drug Effects

Different drugs affect people's bodies in different ways. Stimulants speed up the body, depressants slow down the body, and hallucinogens alter the way people experience things.

Tolerance, dependence, and withdrawal are terms commonly used to describe how people react to alcohol and other drugs.

Psychological Dependence: When a drug is so important in a person's life that it is a focal point for her thoughts, emotions, and activities, the need to continue using the drug becomes a craving or compulsion.

Physical Dependence: When a person's body changes in response to the presence of a drug, withdrawal symptoms occur if she suddenly stops using the drug.

Tolerance: When a person's body becomes used to a drug, more of the drug is needed to produce the desired effects.

Withdrawal Symptoms: When a person who has become physically dependent on a particular drug suddenly stops using the drug, she may experience symptoms ranging from mild to severe discomfort. These symptoms may be the opposite to the effects produced by the drug (e.g., if someone drinks several cups of coffee a day to stay alert, cutting out coffee completely may make her feel extremely tired and lethargic).

In Chapter 6, you can find detailed information on the following substances: alcohol, amphetamines, antidepressants, barbiturates, benzodiazepines, caffeine, cannabis, cocaine, hallucinogens, inhalants, opiates and tobacco.

A Word about Non-Prescription Medication

It is possible to develop problems from the use of medications that can be bought at a drug store without a prescription. Many non-prescription medications (over-the-counter and off-the-shelf) contain mood-altering substances, such as alcohol and codeine.

When making a decision about taking non-prescription medication, it is important for a woman to:
- be aware of what is in the medication
- be aware of both the intended effects and possible side effects of the medication
- take into account what other drugs (e.g., medication, alcohol) she takes
- consult with a pharmacist or physician

Drug Combinations

The risk of drugs interacting with one another or of a person having an adverse drug reaction increases with the number of drugs used. Older people who take more than one drug at a time are at particular risk because of the way their bodies absorb, distribute, metabolize and eliminate drugs.

Drugs that produce similar effects produce stronger effects when two or more drugs are taken together. For example, drinking alcohol while taking benzodiazepines (e.g., for anxiety or for sleeping) may increase sedation effects to dangerous levels. Drugs that produce opposite effects can cancel out the effects of each other when taken together.

Some medications (and illegal drugs) are combinations of different drugs (i.e., they contain several different substances). If a woman is unsure or concerned about the drugs she is taking, she should consult with a pharmacist or physician.

You can find more detailed information about how drugs interact with one another (e.g., alcohol with tobacco) in Chapter 6.

How Do Alcohol and Other Drugs Specifically Affect Women's Bodies?

Much of our knowledge about how the human body works and, more specifically, about how the human body is affected by alcohol and other drugs, is based on men's bodies, men's experience, and research conducted on men. This knowledge is then assumed to apply to the human body and the human experience in general.

Most of the focus on women's bodies is centred around women's reproductive role in society — with the focus of concern being on the health of the fetus and children (e.g., alcohol-related birth effects) rather than on women's health. As a result, much of what we know about the effects of alcohol and other drugs on women's bodies is limited to issues related to women's reproductive health.

There are many ways in which the use of alcohol and other drugs affect women and men in a similar manner. But there are also significant ways in which the effects of substances on women and men differ. There are gender differences in body composition (e.g., fat/water ratio), metabolism, hormones, monthly cycles, and lifetime stages of the body's development. Being aware of these differences has important implications for preventing and treating problematic substance use in women.

It is particularly important to note that the effects of alcohol and other drugs are more pronounced in older women. As the body ages, bodily processes slow down. Alcohol and other drugs remain

in the body for a longer period of time and their effects on the body
are stronger.

Alcohol and other drugs specifically affect women's bodies in the following ways:

Body Composition	It takes less alcohol to affect women than men because: • women's bodies are generally smaller than men's • women's bodies contain less water than men's • women metabolize alcohol at a slower rate than men *As a result:* • alcohol is less diluted in women's bodies • women feel the effects of alcohol sooner (e.g., become drunk on less alcohol) • women's bodies take longer to get rid of alcohol • women develop problems related to alcohol use — and develop more severe symptoms (e.g., cirrhosis of the liver) — within a shorter period Women's bodies retain some medications longer than men's bodies do. Women have more fat in their bodies than men have and some medications, in particular benzodiazepines (e.g., diazepam [Valium]), are fat-soluble. Therefore, they are excreted more slowly and stay in a woman's body for a longer period of time. This effect becomes even more pronounced as women get older.
Health Risks	Women substance users are at increased risk for developing certain health problems. For example, women smokers are more likely than non-smoking women to have osteoporosis, diabetes, cardiovascular disease, hypertension, stroke, and heart disease; and they are more likely than men smokers to develop lung problems (e.g., lung cancer).

Menstrual Cycle	Women's bodies react differently to alcohol depending upon the phase of the menstrual cycle. • the effects of alcohol vary throughout the menstrual cycle, with the highest blood-alcohol levels occurring during the premenstrual phase • women who are trying to stay sober are more likely to relapse when they are experiencing premenstrual syndrome (PMS); they may drink alcohol to ease or eliminate unpleasant PMS symptoms (e.g., depression, irritability, edginess, decreased energy, sleep disruption, forgetfulness, headaches, joint pains)
Reproductive System	Women who use alcohol and other drugs may experience problems related to their reproductive systems. • women who drink heavily experience more gynecological problems (e.g., irregular menstrual cycles, infertility, miscarriages, stillbirths, premature births) and damage to their reproductive systems (e.g., failure to menstruate, problems with their ovaries, failure to ovulate) than women who are light or moderate drinkers • women taking certain substances (e.g., heroin, cocaine) tend to have irregular menstrual periods — this may be partly due to their erratic lifestyle • women smokers who take birth control pills are at increased risk for having a stroke, heart attack and other circulatory diseases • women smokers are likely to experience menopause one to two years earlier than non-smokers
Pregnancy	Drinking heavily or taking other drugs while pregnant can harm a woman's body as well as the developing fetus. • women who drink heavily while they are pregnant are more likely to have miscarriages,

Pregnancy
continued ...

stillbirths and premature births; there is also a chance that the fetus might be born with alcohol-related birth effects (e.g., intellectual disability, shorter height, lower weight, facial deformities, heart defects); heavy drinking by a woman's male partner may also affect the fetus since **alcohol** lowers the sperm count and contributes to the development of abnormal sperm

- the use of **benzodiazepines** (e.g., for anxiety, problems sleeping) while a woman is pregnant may cause the newborn baby to experience withdrawal symptoms; benzodiazepines also pass through a breastfeeding woman's milk to her newborn baby

- using **cannabis** while pregnant can slow down the growth of the fetus and produce mild withdrawal symptoms in the newborn baby

- taking **cocaine** (or crack) while pregnant may result in the placenta separating from the uterus — causing severe hemorrhaging in the woman and the possible death of the fetus; the woman may also go into labor prematurely; cocaine can also affect the growth of the fetus and affect a child's neural development for up to five years after birth

- women dependent on **heroin** are more likely to develop complications during pregnancy and childbirth — they have an unusually high rate of miscarriage, breech delivery, caesarean birth and premature birth; women going through withdrawal from heroin are more likely to have fetuses that are stillborn; and babies born to women who are dependent on heroin are smaller than average, often have serious infections, are likely to exhibit withdrawal symptoms, and have a higher than average death rate

- taking **LSD** during pregnancy may increase a woman's risk of having a miscarriage

14.

Pregnancy
continued ...

- smoking **tobacco** while pregnant can lead to a number of complications: for the woman, there is a greater risk of tubal pregnancy, miscarriage, stillbirth and premature delivery; for the fetus, there is a greater likelihood of growth retardation and oral clefting; and the newborn baby is more likely to have a lower birth weight, to experience Sudden Infant Death Syndrome (SIDS), and to develop illnesses of the lower respiratory tract during the first five years of life

but ...

- some women may need to take **medication** for their overall health (and the health of the fetus) even though they are pregnant; however, it is important that women only take such medication on the advice of a physician

UNDERSTANDING THE INFLUENCES ON WOMEN'S SUBSTANCE USE

Many factors influence whether and for what reasons a woman will choose to use alcohol and other drugs as well as how much she will choose to use. These factors can be broken down into three interdependent categories:

(1) individual influences — characteristics that are unique to each woman (e.g., her personality, behavior, life situation) but may be affected by interpersonal, community, societal and environmental influences

(2) interpersonal and community influences — relationships and situations that fall within a woman's social situation (e.g., social norms, family)

(3) societal and environmental influences — a broad range of factors that could affect all women in society (e.g., laws, marketing practices)

15.

Women's substance use can be a way of coping. The coping strategies that a woman uses are based on her personal characteristics as well as on the interpersonal, community, societal and environmental influences in her life.

In the following diagram depicting the many influences on a woman's life, it is important to remember that each circle has a direct impact on all the circles that fall inside it.

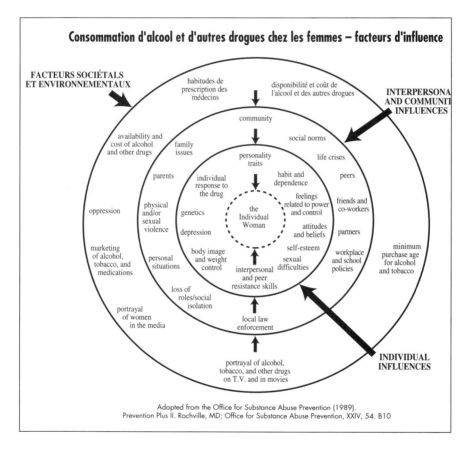

Adapted from the Office for Substance Abuse Prevention (1989). Prevention Plus II. Rochville, MD; Office for Substance Abuse Prevention, XXIV, 54. B10

Some women do not use alcohol or other drugs at all. It may be a matter of availability, cost, lifestyle, for health reasons, because of religious beliefs or cultural practices, different coping strategies, or the fear of developing a problem (particularly if the family has a history of substance use difficulties). Or it may just be that they do not like the way alcohol or other drugs taste or make them feel.

Some women drink alcohol and use other drugs because of the pleasure they get from doing so. Societal norms support the use of substances in this way. Women may drink, smoke or use other drugs to relax, to take a break, to loosen up, to feel more powerful, or to feel high. Most women who use alcohol or other drugs do not develop problems because of their use.

Some women may use alcohol and other drugs to numb their feelings around negative emotions, conflicts and pains over which they feel they have no control — stress, boredom, depression, hormonal changes, low self-esteem, secondary status, social isolation, sexuality issues, being the caregiver with no one to take care of them, lack of money, lack of a support network, lack of control over their lives, violence, loss or stressful life events. But substance use can reinforce and intensify the same negative feelings that women are trying to free themselves of.

Note: The following sections describing the factors that influence women's substance use focus mainly on women who develop problems or become dependent on substances because that is the primary focus of the research and clinical literature on this topic.

Individual Influences

Attitudes and Beliefs

A woman's attitudes and beliefs about a substance and its effects will influence her use or non-use of the substance.

Body Image and Weight Control

Many women have issues around food and eating. Some women are compulsive eaters or overeaters; some have anorexia nervosa or bulimia nervosa (90 per cent of Canadians with anorexia and bulimia are women).

There is a strong association between bulimia and substance use — and many shared characteristics between bulimic women and women who are dependent on alcohol. These include:
- increased depression, impulsiveness, anxiety, social withdrawal, incidence of disturbed childhood and sexual violence, difficulty in coping with stress, lower self-esteem

17.

- the substance (food, alcohol) is used as a way of controlling some aspect of a woman's life — for example, when a woman feels she has little or no control over her life, she may binge (overeat) to comfort herself and purge (vomit, take laxatives or diuretics) to keep her weight down; or she may depend on alcohol or other drugs to comfort herself, numb her feelings, or lose her inhibitions enough to take more control of her life (e.g., by saying what she really thinks instead of not being comfortable doing so)

With society's emphasis on women's physical appearance, many women learn to place more value on the way they look than on their health. Some women use drugs as diet aids in an attempt to keep their weight down. Drugs most commonly used in this way include:
- prescription drugs (appetite suppressants, thyroid hormone)
- over-the-counter medications (diet pills, laxatives, diuretics, emetics, enemas)
- illegal drugs (cocaine)
- tobacco — fear of gaining weight is one of the main barriers to women quitting smoking

Depression and Anxiety

Factors that contribute to depression in women can also lead to women using alcohol and other drugs to cope. Such factors include double standards for men and women, the lack of power and control that women have over some aspects of their lives, and social and economic barriers that limit women's choices.

Depression is more common in women than in men. Theories about why this is the case point to the social context of women's lives and how it affects women's self-esteem and self-concept. They also suggest that social sanctions against women expressing their anger result either in women repressing many of their true feelings or in blaming themselves.

Depression is connected to alcohol dependence in women. It can be difficult to know which came first — depression or alcohol dependence — because the symptoms of primary depression are similar to those of depression brought on by heavy alcohol use. But it is more often the case that depression comes before, or leads to, alcohol dependence in women (the reverse is true for men).

Depression has also been linked to other dependent behaviors in women — smoking, other drug dependence, eating issues, compulsive sexual behavior, and gambling.

Women are often prescribed benzodiazepines for anxiety or stress. If a woman is dependent on alcohol — and the prescribing physician does not ask about or is not aware of it — she could become dependent on both drugs and experience problems due to the interaction between the drugs.

Feelings Related to Power and Control

Dependence on alcohol and other drugs often results from a feeling of powerlessness. Using alcohol and other drugs can create a feeling of power and control that is otherwise lacking in some women's lives.

Many women say that smoking is one way they cope with stress. It is not surprising, then, that women who have less power and control (e.g., those with low incomes, who are unemployed, or have been subjected to violence) are more likely than other women to smoke.

Although the use of alcohol and other drugs may help some women cope in the short term, long-term use of alcohol and other drugs takes away their power by reducing the options available to them and by limiting their ability to think clearly and take action.

Genetics

People with an alcohol-dependent parent may be genetically predisposed to developing alcohol dependence, depending on the presence of other factors.

Habit and Dependence

Using substances can be a habit. It might include having a coffee in the morning, a drink with co-workers after work, or a cigarette to relax after dinner. For some people, continued heavy use may lead to dependence on using the substance for its rewarding or reinforcing effects (e.g., having a coffee to get going in the morning, taking medication to help them sleep). Once they are dependent on a substance, they may experience withdrawal symptoms if they stop using it.

19.

Individual Response to the Drug

Both women and men report that the main reasons they drink alcohol are to be sociable, to enjoy meals, to relax, and to feel good. Similarly, the main reasons they use marijuana are to feel high, to relax, to see what it is like, and to be sociable.

Self-Esteem

Alcohol- and drug-dependent women typically report low self-esteem and a negative self-image. Alcohol and other drugs can temporarily provide a heightened sense of self-worth, but often the shame and guilt that follow their use result in lowered self-esteem.

Sexual Difficulties

Sexual difficulties (e.g., lack of erotic feelings or interest, lack of sexual arousal or pleasure, painful intercourse, lack of lubrication, lack of orgasm) lead some women to drink heavily. However, heavy drinking may increase sexual difficulties for some women. The real cause of sexual difficulties in some women may be previous or current sexual violence, physical health problems or depression

Alcohol-dependent women often report that they drink to feel comfortable having sex. In fact, some women have never experienced sex without using alcohol or other drugs (e.g., because they may associate sex with violence in their lives).

Interpersonal and Societal Influences

Family Issues

Women with alcohol and other drug problems are more likely to come from a family environment in which some of the following characteristics were present:

- parental lack of attention, nurturing, security and safety for the child; inconsistent parenting, emotional distancing in the parents, parental separation or divorce, and sexual and other forms of family violence
- pressure to conform to normative or traditional forms of behavior (e.g., dependence, compliance) for women

To compensate for this type of upbringing, some women find that they gain a sense of independence, reduce their inhibitions, and express themselves more freely when they use alcohol or illegal drugs.

Alcohol-dependent women are more likely than alcohol-dependent men to have an alcohol-dependent parent — and they are also more likely than other women to marry an alcohol-dependent man.

Life Crises

Many women report that their problematic use of alcohol and other drugs is directly related to a specific crisis (e.g., birth of a child, a separation or divorce, the death of a loved one) in their lives. Most life crises are losses of some kind — loss of a partner (through divorce or death), loss of a job, loss of roles (e.g., children leaving home, retirement, moving because of a partner's job) and loss of culture.

Loss of Roles/Social Isolation
(a) Women Living in Poverty

Women living in poverty have fewer financial resources and fewer choices in their lives. They lack the necessities of life — they have reduced access to housing, education, jobs and health care — and have limited opportunities to improve their life situation. In addition, society frequently views low-income people negatively. All these factors cause psychological stress in low-income women and may lead them to use alcohol or other drugs to cope.

Women who are dependent on alcohol or other drugs find it difficult to stop or reduce their use of substances. For women living in poverty, spending the little money they have on substances, in order to cope, leaves even less money for other things, such as food, clothing and shelter.

Limited economic resources become an issue if women who develop an alcohol or drug problem want to get help — they may need money to pay for transportation and child care, and may not be paid when they take time off work.

(b) Single Mothers

Women raising children without a partner are usually under more stress and have fewer resources than other women. They may attend to their children's needs but neglect their own. And some single parents may cope with the additional stresses they face by using alcohol and other drugs.

21.

(c) Older Women

As women get older, they face a number of social, economic and biological changes that, for some women, may be stressful. These include loss of a partner, social isolation and lack of support. These changes can affect an older woman's self-concept, thus reducing her self-esteem and self-respect. They also increase the likelihood that an older woman could become dependent on alcohol or medications as a way of coping with the changes and losses facing her at this stage of her life.

Older women metabolize substances more slowly; thus drugs remain in their bodies for a longer period of time. Yet more drugs are prescribed for older women than for any other group and most drug problems in older women result from taking legal (over-the-counter and prescription) drugs.

(d) Immigrant and Refugee Women

Many immigrant and refugee women experience social isolation, heightened by language and cultural barriers, when they come to Canada. Some immigrant and refugee women may develop problems with alcohol or other drugs in response to discrimination, lack of meaningful work, an identity crisis trying to fit into Canadian society, and cultural conflicts at home. Refugee women may suffer from post-traumatic stress disorder as a result of having witnessed, or endured, violence and torture in their home countries. Difficulty in communicating with health professionals may also result in women receiving either wrong or unnecessary prescriptions.

(e) Aboriginal Women

Aboriginal women continue to live with the consequences of cultural oppression and past physical and sexual violence in residential schools. These actions led to the breakdown of aboriginal people's traditional lifestyle, cultural practices, values and self-esteem, and left a legacy in aboriginal communities where acts of violence and problematic use of alcohol and other drugs are often the norm.

Aboriginal women often perceive alcohol and other drug use and suicide as the most effective ways to cope with the realities of their daily lives and their lack of hope for a better future.

22.

Aboriginal women list low self-esteem, poor
lack of control in their lives as the main reasons
dependence on alcohol and other drugs.

(f) Lesbians and Bisexual Women

Many lesbians and bisexual women hide their sexual orientation due
to negative societal attitudes toward gays and lesbians. Many are concerned that they could lose their jobs or have their children taken from
them if people know they are lesbians. Many become isolated within
the larger society and often feel the need to lead a "double life".

Anti-lesbian attitudes and discriminating practices in society,
together with the internalization of these attitudes, contribute to the
onset of problematic drinking and other drug use among lesbians
and bisexual women.

Bars were once one of the few meeting places for lesbians and
bisexual women. This situation is changing, however, with the
increased visibility of gays and lesbians in larger urban centres.
Now there are numerous gay and lesbian social, political and religious clubs and organizations where lesbians and bisexual women
can meet. In small or rural communities, however, there are likely
to be limited or no social supports.

(g) Homeless Women

The use of alcohol and other drugs is common among people living
on the street — and substances are available and easy to obtain.

Being poor and homeless increases the likelihood of women
using alcohol and other drugs to cope with the realities of their experiences and with life on the street.

Homeless women who are alcohol- or drug-dependent are more
likely than other women to experience violence (e.g., being beaten
or raped) in their lives. Having to cope with the violence reinforces
their use of alcohol and other drugs.

(h) Women with Disabilities

Women with disabilities must cope with negative societal attitudes
about people with disabilities — in a culture that values physical perfection, especially for women. On the other hand, societal attitudes
may encourage or ignore problem use of alcohol and other drugs

among women with disabilities (e.g., "I would drink too if I were in her position.")

Women with disabilities may face barriers in day-to-day living. They are more likely to be unemployed, have fewer economic resources, and face discrimination and physical and societal barriers that make them more isolated and increase their likelihood of becoming dependent on alcohol or other drugs. Attending treatment programs can also be difficult if facilities lack wheelchair access, interpreters are not available, etc.

Women with disabilities are more likely to take alcohol or other drugs to try to cope with their problems if they are in chronic pain, have difficulty sleeping, or are angry or lonely.

Women with disabilities are more likely to experience emotional, physical and sexual violence than other women, increasing the likelihood that they will use alcohol and other drugs to cope with the violence.

(i) Women who Work in Certain Occupations
The drinking levels of women become similar to those of men when women work with men in traditional male occupations where levels of alcohol use are high.

Women who work in the sex trade (especially prostitutes) may have high rates of alcohol and other drug use. Some women in the sex trade have experienced sexual violence as children and use alcohol and other drugs to cope with their feelings. And some use alcohol and other drugs before going to work to numb their feelings while working. Women in the sex trade may also be at risk for sexually transmitted infections through sharing needles or having unprotected sex.

Peer Pressure
Peer pressure from a woman's friends, colleagues or partner may influence her to experiment with or use more of a particular substance.

Personal Situations
Some women use alcohol and other drugs to cope with negative life circumstances. These may include situations in their family as they were growing up, issues in their relationships with partners, personal factors (e.g., self-esteem, aging, loss, body image), and being isolated within society.

24.

Physical and/or Sexual Violence

Women who have experienced physical and/or sexual violence at some time in their lives are more likely than other women to take medication (e.g., for anxiety or to help them sleep) and to be dependent on alcohol or other drugs.

Childhood sexual violence can be linked with subsequent sexual difficulties and problematic substance use as an adult. Experiencing childhood sexual violence or other forms of family violence leads some women to numb their feelings and their pain with alcohol and other drugs.

Physical and/or sexual violence affects women in many ways, including the following:

- women may develop feelings of shame, worthlessness and low self-esteem
- women may be unsure about setting limits and boundaries (e.g., a woman may find it difficult to say "no")
- women may have difficulty forming intimate relationships
- women may develop self-harming behaviors (e.g., slashing their skin)
- women may be afraid of sexual contact since it can activate memories and feelings of the past violence
- women may take alcohol and other drugs to block out their thoughts and feelings about the violence, to deal with physical and emotional pain, to cope with their fears, or to feel in control; women who continue to do so may eventually develop a dependence on the drug(s) they are taking

Social Norms

In general, the use of certain substances is a common, socially acceptable practice in Canadian society. Cultural, community and family norms may also influence a person's choice and use of drugs. One example would be the heavier use of alcohol by younger people. For example, heavy-drinking occasions are most common among young people in their late teens and early twenties and young people are generally more tolerant of people becoming intoxicated. Women generally drink less than men and tend to be less tolerant of people becoming intoxicated.

Women with Partners

Alcohol-dependent women are more likely to have alcohol-dependent partners than are alcohol-dependent men. And men are more likely than women to leave an alcohol-dependent partner.

Women who use illegal drugs are often introduced to the drugs and supplied drugs by men with whom they have an intimate relationship.

Alcohol- and drug-dependent women who want to get treatment for their dependency often are not supported in their actions by their substance-using partner if their partner is not interested in treatment.

Women whose partners are physically or sexually violent are more likely than other women to use alcohol and other drugs to cope with injuries and feelings brought on by the violence. And alcohol-dependent women are subjected to more violence by their partners than are other women.

Environmental Influences

Marketing Drugs to Women

Advertisements for champagne, wine and cocktails are designed to increase women's use of alcohol.

Tobacco advertising stresses the changing roles in women's lives, the social acceptability of women's smoking, the link between smoking and weight control, and women's independence, sophistication, success, youth and health.

Drug companies market their products to women through advertising directed at physicians. Advertisements tend to portray women as more emotional than men and suggest that drugs will help women cope with these feelings. This may be one reason why women are more likely than men to receive prescriptions for, and to use, mood-altering drugs.

Oppression

Having to deal with systemic issues — social expectations, sexism, racism, harassment, discrimination, assault — is a constant source of stress for many women. It influences how women are treated in their families, in their communities, in the workplace, and by health and social service providers. It also affects how women feel about themselves and what they believe their options are in coping with issues in their lives. Substance use is one option which some women choose.

Compared to men, the average woman earns less money, has fewer or no work benefits (since she is more likely to work part time), and does more of the unpaid work. As a result, women have less time and fewer options to take care of themselves.

Physicians' Prescribing Practices

The medical profession can be another source of women's drug use.

- it is socially acceptable to prescribe drugs to women for anxiety and depression — but the cause of these symptoms is often overlooked or ignored; this reinforces the use of drugs to cope with problems rather than confronting the problems themselves
- general practitioners and psychiatrists prescribe twice as many mood-altering drugs (e.g., for depression, anxiety and sleep problems) for women as they do for men
- physicians do not always take the time to discuss other coping mechanisms than medication (e.g., eating habits, exercise, relaxation)
- women who receive medical care from more than one physician may receive prescriptions that the other physician(s) are unaware of; this could result in women obtaining (and taking) medication in larger amounts than recommended or in being prescribed medications that should not be taken together
- there is a power imbalance between physician and patient, which, together with women's socialization not to be assertive, contributes to women not playing an active role in deciding on the medicine they receive and take

HOW WOMEN USE: PATTERNS OF WOMEN'S SUBSTANCE USE

Contemporary Patterns of Substance Use among Women in Canada

Research studies have examined the substance use of a variety of populations (e.g., national, provincial, adults, students). These studies

27.

show that women's alcohol and other drug use depend on a number of factors including their age, family history and stresses (daily and specific events) in their lives.

General Patterns of Substance Use among Women

Alcohol is the drug most commonly used by women.

- approximately 67 per cent of Canadian women are current drinkers [Health Canada, 1995]
- the percentage of women drinkers is lowest in the eastern provinces and the highest in the West (from a low of 57 per cent in Prince Edward Island to a high of 81 per cent in British Columbia) [Eliany et al, 1990]
- drinking is related to income: 52 per cent of Canadian women earning less than $10,000 drink alcohol compared to 86 per cent of women earning $40,000 or more [Eliany et al, 1990]
- Canadian women tend to drink less as they get older

Twenty-six per cent of Canadian women smoke cigarettes. [Health Canada, 1995]

- 28 per cent of female students in Grades 7 to 13 in Ontario report that they smoke [Adlaf et al, 1995]

In a national survey looking at drug use in the past 12 months: [Health Canada, 1995]

- 14 per cent of Canadian women used prescription pain medication
- 5 per cent of Canadian women reported using sleeping pills (benzodiazepines)
- 5 per cent of Canadian women took tranquillizers (benzodiazepines)
- 5 per cent of Canadian women reported using cannabis
- 4 per cent of Canadian women reported taking antidepressants

Three per cent of women have used cocaine or crack at some time during their lives. [Eliany et al, 1990]

28.

Patterns of Substance Use among Specific Subgroups of Women

Certain groups of women may have substance use patterns that differ from the general population of women.

- girls who are concerned about their weight are twice as likely to smoke as girls who do not have the same concerns
- women with fewer social and work roles are more likely to develop drinking-related problems; this may be due to the fact that having multiple roles (including paid employment) enhances women's self-esteem, gives them greater access to social support networks, and decreases their likelihood of developing mental health problems
- women who view their lives as being stressful are more likely to take aspirins and pain relievers; current drinkers are also more likely than non-drinkers to take these drugs
- women who experienced physical and/or sexual violence as children and/or as adults are more likely than other women to take medication (e.g., benzodiazepines for anxiety or to help them sleep)
- treatment program staff report that 40 to 80 per cent of women who enter their programs for alcohol and other drug problems have experienced physical or sexual violence at some time during their lives
- women who are smokers or ex-smokers tend to drink more than other women; in treatment programs for alcohol dependency, for example, most women are likely to be smokers
- women who are heavy drinkers are more likely than other women to be dependent on other drugs and are more likely to have partners who are also heavy drinkers
- women entering treatment programs are often dependent on both alcohol and mood-altering medications
- older women (65 years of age and over) are more likely than younger women to use prescription (e.g., benzodiazepines for sleeping and anxiety) and over-the-counter medications, are less likely to use alcohol and tobacco, and rarely use illicit drugs
- older women who have less education, less money, poorer health, and are under stress are more likely to be given prescriptions to help them sleep and for anxiety

How Women's Substance Use Differs from Men's

Alcohol and other drug use by women, as compared to men, varies in a number of significant ways. These include the reasons for using substances, the type of drugs most commonly used, and the patterns of use.

Compared to Men, Women are More Likely to...

Women are twice as likely to use legal, mood-altering drugs (over-the-counter and prescription medications). These include benzodiazepines (for anxiety and sleep problems) and opiates (e.g., codeine, demerol, morphine) for pain.

Women are twice as likely to receive prescriptions from their doctors for mood-altering drugs that are designed to treat symptoms of anxiety, depression and insomnia.
- physicians more often perceive women's problems to be related to their emotions and thus are more likely to prescribe benzodiazepines and antidepressants for women
- women are more likely than men to visit their doctor when they have an emotion-related problem, such as anxiety, tension or depression

Women are more likely to drink alcohol and take mood-altering prescription drugs at the same time.

Alcohol-dependent women in treatment are more likely to have developed a dependence on other drugs before developing a dependence on alcohol; for men the reverse is true.

Compared to Men, Women are Less Likely to ...

Women tend to drink less alcohol (per occasion, per week) than men.

Women are less likely than men to drink alcohol daily.

Women are less likely than men to use illegal drugs.

30.

NEGATIVE STEREOTYPES ABOUT WOMEN'S SUBSTANCE USE

Negative stereotypes about women who drink heavily or use certain drugs come from the double standards for women and men that are prevalent in society, and from social and cultural expectations that women are responsible for certain roles within the family.

Women are expected to strive for and achieve a higher moral standard than men. As a result, women who are dependent on alcohol or illegal drugs are viewed in a more negative way than are alcohol- or drug-dependent men.

- risk-taking and unconventional behaviors are admired more in men than in women (i.e., they are seen as being less acceptable for women)
- men who go to bars or become intoxicated are generally viewed as acting in a natural and socially acceptable way; women who do the same tend to be viewed as unattractive, promiscuous and as behaving in an unfeminine manner
- women who are heavy drinkers or illegal drug users are viewed as being sicker, morally weaker, and more deviant than are their male counterparts
- women's substance use is seen as shameful, while men's alcohol and other drug use is used as an excuse for their behavior

Alcohol- and drug-dependence in women is seen as a threat to women fulfilling their multiple caregiver roles.

- societal values condone men taking time out from other responsibilities (e.g., going to a bar after work) but view women's job of taking care of children and others as a full-time responsibility
- women are viewed as not doing their job properly if they are not busy taking care of people with whom they have relationships

Women who are dependent on alcohol or illegal drugs are believed to be sexually aggressive and promiscuous. But women who are heavy users of alcohol and other drugs are actually more likely to have sexually-aggressive acts done to them.

As a result of these stereotypes:

There is a stigma against women who have a substance use problem.

- this makes it more difficult for a woman to admit to herself and to others that she has a substance use problem (e.g., a woman may fear that others will label her as a "bad" partner and mother); so she may try to hide her substance use or downplay it
- substance-using women internalize these negative stereotypes; they are more likely to feel ashamed or guilty about their substance use (e.g., they may feel they are failing in their roles as partners and mothers), which has a negative effect on their self-esteem and can lead to increased substance use

Often women (as well as their family and friends) downplay their substance use and do not consider it a problem. They are more likely to say they are depressed, have problems in their relationships, etc. As a result, a woman will often not go for help until she faces a crisis — and even then is more likely to seek help from a health professional (e.g., physician, mental health worker) who is also less likely to recognize her problems with substance use and may prescribe medications that intensify her problems.

Women who have problems with substance use may experience more violence in their lives.

- there is more social acceptance for violence that is directed against people whose behavior society has labelled as unacceptable
- there is the belief that a woman who drinks to excess or takes illegal drugs deserves whatever happens to her, especially while under the influence of drugs

Some counsellors believe that women do not do as well as men in treatment. But it really depends on the treatment. Many treatment programs have been developed for men and do not address women's needs and issues. As a result, women do better in some treatment programs than in others.

UNDERSTANDING DIFFERENT THEORETICAL AND PHILOSOPHICAL APPROACHES

A number of theories and conceptual approaches look at alcohol and other drug use. Each approach offers its own perspective on the cause of dependence or problematic substance use, the best way to treat it, and the goal of treatment.

The most common approaches are the disease/medical approach, cognitive-behavioral approach, biopsychosocial approach, and harm-reduction approach. The basic concepts of each approach are outlined in the table on the following page.

Many treatment programs in Canada use the disease/medical approach to some degree. This may range from including "12-step" work as a program component to requiring clients to attend mutual aid groups (e.g., Alcoholics Anonymous) while receiving treatment.

APPROACH	BELIEF SYSTEM	REASONS FOR PROBLEMS	RECOMMENDED INTERVENTION
BIOPSYCHOSOCIAL	• anyone can develop a substance use problem • problematic substance use results from the combination of biological, psychological and sociocultural factors	• individual characteristics combine with environmental factors to produce behaviors that could be progressively self-harming	• no single treatment approach is appropriate for all people • a wide range of treatment options should be available • it is best to match the client with treatment that most closely meets her needs, strengths and situation
COGNITIVE-BEHAVIORAL	• one must look at the individual's belief system (cognitive factor), her environment (behavioral factor), and the relationship between the two to understand and be able to treat her substance use problems	• people's belief systems regarding substance use (e.g., society approves of substance use, alcohol and other drugs have positive effects, substances help people cope with negative emotions or situations) • continued use can lead to negative consequences (e.g., tolerance, dependence)	• strive for abstinence and/or reduced drinking • help the client take responsibility for her behavior • through behavioral skill training show the client other ways to cope • help the client change her attitude and lifestyle
DISEASE/MEDICAL	• dependence on alcohol or other drugs is a disease • users are often "in denial" and are not ready to address their substance use problem or make a change until they "hit bottom"	• genetic factors play a key role in the development of substance use problems • the disease continues to get worse and the person is no longer able to control her use	• abstinence (stopping use of the drug forever) is the only way to halt the progress of the disease and recover from its effects
HARM REDUCTION	• substance use cannot be totally eliminated but the harm related to substance use can be reduced	• alcohol and other drug use is normal in society • there are benefits as well as risks from substance use	• the goal is reduced use of substances or abstinence • identify and deal with harmful behaviors in a practical way • focus on immediate and achievable change • education • policy-making • health promotion

Woman-Centred Approach

This guidebook uses an approach that blends the biopsychosocial, cognitive-behavioral and harm-reduction approaches.

Cognitive-behavioral
provides us with the tools to help women make lifestyle changes. It focuses on how a woman sees herself, the substance, and the role it plays in her life. It helps a woman look at how self-talk influences her substance use and teaches her how to challenge her thinking processes (e.g., self-defeating ideas). It looks at how a woman views alternatives to coping with life situations and how she views issues of self-esteem and self-efficacy.

WOMEN

Harm reduction
provides us with the methods to help women reduce the problems associated with their substance use. It targets specific, well-defined, harmful behaviors.

Biopsychosocial
provides us with a viewpoint that sees women as individuals within the context of the larger society. It enables us to understand what it is like to be both a woman and a substance user within our society; and to examine what treatment is best for the woman at the present time.

The disease/medical approach is often used with the other approaches found in the above model. It is an approach used in many treatment programs across Canada and it is a way of addressing substance use problems that can work well for women with serious alcohol and other drug problems.

35.

REFERENCES

Abbott, Beverley A. (October 30, 1990). *Women and Substance Abuse: Current Knowledge and Treatment Implications.* A Review of the Literature. 29.

Action on Women's Addictions — Research & Education (AWARE). (1995). *Making Connections: A Booklet About Women and Prescription Drugs and Alcohol.* Kingston, ON: AWARE, 34.

Addiction Research Foundation. (1995). *LINK — Violence Against Women and Children in Relationships and the Use of Alcohol and Drugs: Searching for Solutions.* An Educational Package. Toronto: Addiction Research Foundation.

Addiction Research Foundation. (1991). Stats facts: Women. *The Journal,* (June/July):13.

Adlaf, Edward M., Ivis, Frank J. & Smart, Reginald G. (1994) *Alcohol and Other Drug Use Among Ontario Adults in 1994 and Changes Since 1977.* Toronto: Addiction Research Foundation, xviii, 126.

Adlaf, Edward M., Ivis, Frank J., Smart, Reginald G. & Walsh, Gordon W. (1995). *The Ontario Student Drug Use Survey: 1977-1995.* Toronto: Addiction Research Foundation, xxi, 187.

Ashley, Mary Jane. (1995). *The Health Effects of Tobacco Use.* Ottawa: National Clearinghouse on Tobacco and Health, 18.

Blackwell, Judith, Thurston, Wilfreda E. & Graham, Kathryn. (1996). Canadian women and substance use: Overview and policy implications. In Lundy, Colleen, Eliany, Marc & Adrian, Manuella (eds.). *Women's Use of Alcohol and Other Drugs: Special Perspectives from the National Alcohol and Other Drugs Survey.* Toronto: Addiction Research Foundation.

Blume, Sheila B. (1990). Chemical Dependency in Women: Important Issues. *American Journal of Drug and Alcohol Abuse,* 16 (3&4):297-307.

Blume, Sheila B. (1986). Women and Alcohol: A Review. *Journal of the American Medical Association,* 256(11):1467-1470.

Boland, Fred J. (1993). Eating disorders and substance abuse. In Howard, Betty-Anne M., Harrison, Susan, Carver, Virginia & Lightfoot, Lynn (eds.). *Alcohol & Drug Problems: A Practical Guide for Counsellors.* Toronto: Addiction Research Foundation, 363-380.

Bulik, Cynthia M. (1992). Abuse of Drugs Associated with Eating Disorders. *Journal of Substance Abuse,* 4:69-90.

Bullock, Doug. (1993). The physically disabled substance abuser. In Howard, Betty-Anne M., Harrison, Susan, Carver, Virginia & Lightfoot, Lynn (eds.). *Alcohol & Drug Problems: A Practical Guide for Counsellors*. Toronto: Addiction Research Foundation, 219-228.

Coulter, Rebecca. (1993). *Gender Socialization: New Ways, New World*. Working Group of Status of Women Officials on Gender Equity in Education and Training, 16.

Eliany, Marc & Courtemanche, Jean-René. (1992). *Smoking Behavior of Canadians: A National Alcohol and Other Drugs Survey Report (1989)*. Ottawa: Supply and Services Canada, ix, 56.

Eliany, Marc, Giesbrecht, Norman, Nelson, Mike, Wellman, Barry & Wortley, Scot (eds.). (1990). *National Alcohol and Other Drugs Survey: Highlights Report*. Ottawa: Supply and Services Canada, x, 42.

Finkelstein, Norma, Duncan, Sally Anne, Derman, Laura & Smeltz, Janet. (1990). *Getting Sober, Getting Well: A Treatment Guide for Caregivers who Work with Women*. Cambridge, MA: Women's Alcoholism Program of CAS-PAR, xiii, 632.

Forth-Finegan, Jahn L. (1991). Sugar and Spice and Everything Nice: Gender Socialization and Women's Addiction — a literature review. In Bepko, Claudia (ed.). *Feminism and Addiction*. New York: Haworth, 19-48.

Goettler, Darla L. & Pearce, Debbie. (July 1991). *The Many Faces of Women and Substance Use: A Review of the Literature*. Health Canada, 33.

Gomberg, Edith S. Lisansky. (1986). Women: Alcohol and Other Drugs. *Drugs & Society*, 1(1):75-109.

Graham, Kathryn, Carver, Virginia & Brett, Pamela J. (1996).Women aged 65 and Over: Alcohol and Drug Use. In Lundy, Colleen, Eliany, Marc & Adrian, Manuella (eds.). *Women's Use of Alcohol and Other Drugs: Special Perspectives from the National Alcohol and Other Drugs Survey*. Toronto: Addiction Research Foundation.

Groeneveld, Judith & Shain, Martin. (July 1989). *Drug Use among Victims of Physical and Sexual Abuse: A Preliminary Report*. Toronto: Addiction Research Foundation, 9.

Harrison, Susan. (1993). Working with women. In Howard, Betty-Anne M., Harrison, Susan, Carver, Virginia & Lightfoot, Lynn (eds.). *Alcohol & Drug Problems: A Practical Guide for Counsellors*. Toronto: Addiction Research Foundation, 195-218.

Health Canada. (1995). *Canada's Alcohol and Other Drugs Survey, 1994*. Ottawa: Minister of Supply and Services, 6.

37.

Health Canada. (1994). *Working Together: A National Workshop for Action on Women and Substance Use*. Report. Ottawa: 53.

Hill, Shirley Y. (1984). Vulnerability to the biomedical consequences of alcoholism and alcohol-related problems among women. In Wilsnack, Sharon C. & Beckman, Linda J. (eds.). *Alcohol Problems in Women: Antecedents, Consequences and Intervention*. New York: Guilford, 117-120.

Kahan, Meldon. (1993). Physical effects of alcohol and other drugs. In Howard, Betty-Anne M., Harrison, Susan, Carver, Virginia & Lightfoot, Lynn (eds.). *Alcohol & Drug Problems: A Practical Guide for Counsellors*. Toronto: Addiction Research Foundation, 103-117.

LaDue, Robin A. (1991). Coyote returns: Survival for Native American women. In Roth, Paula (ed.). *Alcohol and Drugs are Women's Issues*. Volume One: A Review of the Issues. Metuchen, NJ: Women's Action Alliance and Scarecrow Press, 23-31.

Lundy, Colleen, Carver, Virginia & Pederson, Linda. (1996). Young women: Alcohol, tobacco and other drugs. In Lundy, Colleen, Eliany, Marc & Adrian, Manuella (eds.). *Women's Use of Alcohol and Other Drugs: Special Perspectives from the National Alcohol and Other Drugs Survey*. Toronto: Addiction Research Foundation.

Miller, Brenda A. & Downs, William R. (1993). The Impact of Family Violence on the Use of Alcohol by Women. *Alcohol Health & Research Health*, 17(2):137-143.

Miller, Brenda A., Downs, William R. & Testa, Maria. (1993). Interrelationships Between Victimization Experiences and Women's Alcohol Use. *Journal of Studies on Alcohol*, 11(supp.):109-117.

Mitchinson, Wendy. (1988). The medical treatment of women. In Burt, Sandra, Code, Lorraine & Dorney, Lindsay (eds.). *Changing Patterns: Women in Canada*. Toronto: McClelland and Stewart, 237-261.

Pomerleau, Cynthia S., Berman, Barbara A., Gritz, Ellen R., Marks, Judith L. & Goeters, Susan. (1994). Why women smoke. In Watson, Ronald R. (ed.). *Addictive Behaviors in Women*. Drug and Alcohol Abuse Reviews 5. Totowa, NJ: Humana, 39-70.

Reed, Beth Glover. (1991). Linkages: Battering, sexual assault, incest, child sexual abuse, teen pregnancy, dropping out of school and the alcohol and drug connection. In Roth, Paula (ed.). *Alcohol and Drugs are Women's Issues*. Volume One: A Review of the Issues. Metuchen, NJ: Women's Action Alliance and Scarecrow Press, 130-149.

Reed, Beth Glover. (1985). Drug Misuse and Dependency in Women: The Meaning and Implications of Being Considered a Special Population or Minority Group. *The International Journal of the Addictions*, 20(1):13-62.

Riley, Diane. (No date). *The Harm Reduction Model: Pragmatic Approaches to Drug Use from the Area Between Intolerance and Neglect.* Canadian Centre on Substance Abuse, 16.

Ross, Helen E. (1995) DSM-III-R Alcohol Abuse and Dependence and Psychiatric Comorbidity in Ontario: Results from the Mental Health Supplement to the Ontario Health Survey. *Drug and Alcohol Dependence*, 39, 111-128.

Schuckit, Marc A., Tipp, Jayson E. & Kelner, Erica. (1994). Are Daughters of Alcoholics More Likely to Mmarry Alcoholics? *American Journal of Drug and Alcohol Abuse*, 20(2):237-245.

Scott, Kim. (1996). Canadian indigenous women and substance use. In Lundy, Colleen, Eliany, Marc & Adrian, Manuella (eds.). *Women's Use of Alcohol and Other Drugs: Special Perspectives from the National Alcohol and Other Drugs Survey.* Toronto: Addiction Research Foundation.

Underhill, Brenda L. & Ostermann, Suzanne E. (1991). The Pain of Invisibility: Issues for Lesbians. In Roth, Paula (ed.). *Alcohol and Drugs are Women's Issues. Volume One: A Review of the Issues.* Metuchen, NJ: Women's Action Alliance and Scarecrow Press, 71-77.

Van Den Bergh, Nan. (1991). Having Bitten the Apple: A Feminist Perspective on Addictions. In Van Den Bergh, Nan (ed.). *Feminist Perspectives on Addiction.* New York: Springer, 3-30.

Wilsnack, Sharon C. (1993). *Work, Marriage, Sexuality and Problem Drinking in Women: Findings from a U.S. National Longitudinal Study.* Paper presented at Pre-International Women's Day Forum on Women and Addictions. Toronto: Addiction Research Foundation, 3.

Wilsnack, Sharon C. & Wilsnack, Richard W. (1991). Epidemiology of Women's Drinking. *Journal of Substance Abuse*, 3:133-157.

Zimmer, Rita & Schretzman, Maryanne. (1991). Issues for homeless women and their children. In Roth, Paula (ed.). *Alcohol and Drugs are Women's Issues.* Volume One: A Review of the Issues. Metuchen, NJ: Women's Action Alliance and Scarecrow Press, 173-177.

Important Issues to Consider when Working with Women

INTRODUCTION

The following section addresses some of the areas to consider in selecting a treatment program, and the potential barriers to a woman in accessing programs. If you are planning to refer a woman for more specialized help with an alcohol or other drug problem, or even if you and the client plan to continue to work together, it is important to identify the barriers or issues that may prevent her from participating fully in counselling or treatment.

In deciding with the client on a plan for referral, it may not be possible to address all her issues satisfactorily because the ideal service may not exist. You may need to prioritize with the client what are her most critical issues and together find a service or services that best meet her needs. A lack of choice in services may mean that not all her issues can be addressed. However, it is important to identify the issues and find the best way to address them.

More barriers to treatment exist for women than for men. Some of these barriers are structural (imposed by the woman's environment or the program's environment) while others stem from psychosocial issues (the woman's concerns about how getting help will affect her life and her relationships). Considering these barriers will make it easier for a woman to get and use appropriate help in dealing with her substance use problem.

41.

ACCESS ISSUES

Access for the Disabled

People with disabilities may have more difficulty attending treatment programs. They may need more flexible programming due to lack of access to public transportation or they may need technical aids or interpreters. In some cases, they may need to go out of town for specialized programs.

Check with your local information centre for resources within your own community. For more specialized programs, check with your provincial addictions agency or Ministry of Health.

Age

Although in recent years treatment components or full programs have been developed to address the needs of specific age groups (e.g., adolescents, older adults), these may only be available in larger urban centres. Older women and younger women may share a common concern that their age-specific issues will not be addressed or that they may have to leave their home community to attend a program. Some older women may also have difficulty participating in treatment programs because of hearing or sight impairments or because of physical mobility problems. Explore with the client any concerns she may have around these issues and try to address them before she enters a program.

Child Care

Women are usually the main caregivers for their children. For a woman to enter treatment, arrangements must be made for care of her children in an appropriate, safe setting. Partners and/or family may not be safe settings because they may have substance use problems themselves or may be emotionally, physically or sexually violent. A woman may also be afraid of using children's and family services for temporary care because she may fear that her children will be taken from her.

The percentage of women is higher in treatment programs that provide child care, but such programs are rare. Therefore, it is important to have information about available child care resources and a good relationship with a worker at local children's and family services who is knowledgeable about substance use issues and is sensitive to a woman's concerns about losing her children.

Detoxification

Many treatment programs require that women be substance-free or detoxified before starting the program. This detoxification may take two to three days for alcohol and many street drugs, but may be much longer for women taking psychoactive medication, such as benzodiazepines. Some women will be able to stop using substances on their own, while others may need to be referred to a detoxification centre or to withdraw from medications under the supervision of a physician.

Finances

More women than men have part-time jobs, receive less pay, and have fewer benefits and less job security. Taking time to go for treatment — whether residential or outpatient — can mean loss of pay, as well as possible loss of the job itself. Paying for child care or care for other family members may be an additional expense that a woman cannot afford.

In some cases, social benefit payments are directed towards covering living costs in long-term residential treatment centres. In such cases, a woman may lose her home because she does not have money to pay the rent while she is in residential treatment.

Lack of Support from Family and Friends

A woman's partner, family members and friends often deny that a woman has a substance use problem and discourage her from seeking treatment. Or, if a woman does start a treatment program, she may leave the program early because of pressure or threats from her partner.

It is important to check with a woman to find what kind of support she has from her partner, family or friends. Some questions you could ask her include the following:

- Is your partner (family member, friend) going to continue to drink and/or use drugs?
- Does your partner understand what is involved when a person goes for substance use treatment?

- Will your partner support your goal of reducing your substance use or being abstinent?
- Can you ask your partner for help when you need it?

Evidence suggests that even if one friend or family member can be identified and actively involved to give social support on an ongoing basis, the client will do better in treatment.

Language Barriers and Lack of Culturally-Sensitive Services

Language is a major barrier for women who do not speak English. They are not likely to use health services unless there is a crisis and then find they have difficulty explaining their problem. This makes it more difficult for physicians, for example, to accurately diagnose the problem and to prescribe appropriate medication. It also means that these women are not likely to seek help until their health problem is at a more advanced stage.

Substance use services that are culturally sensitive and/or offered in languages other than English are difficult to find. Even when a woman does find services in the language she speaks, the services may not be women-sensitive.

If an agency indicates that it offers substance use counselling in certain languages or for people from specific ethnocultural groups, find out if this service is always available before you refer a woman. It may be an ongoing service or it may just reflect the language skills or experience of one staff member.

In some larger communities, it may be possible to arrange for a translator to accompany a woman attending a treatment program or seeing a counsellor on an individual basis. It may not be appropriate for a family member to provide translation.

Location of the Program

A woman may have to travel some distance in her community to attend a treatment program or she may have to leave her community for some services, particularly residential services. You will need to find out if she has transportation and/or has enough money for transportation.

44.

Mood-Altering Prescription Medication

Programs often have admission policies regarding the use of prescribed, mood-altering medication. This may depend on their location and staff (e.g., community-based with no physician attached to the program versus hospital-based with a physician as part of the program staff) as well as on their program philosophy (e.g., they may view all mood-altering medications as being addictive).

Most programs require that clients not use benzodiazepines (medications for anxiety and sleeping problems) while they participate in a group program. However, they may see a woman for individual counselling or support while she is withdrawing from such medications.

Some programs do not accept women who are using antidepressants. This is particularly true if program staff believe that the antidepressants are being prescribed to address societal problems rather than to deal with a depression caused by a chemical imbalance.

Some programs will also not accept women who are taking medications for mental health problems (e.g., bipolar disorder, psychosis). A woman's admission into a program may be decided on an individual basis, depending on her circumstances and the attitudes and skills of the staff about mental health problems.

PROGRAM ISSUES

Concerns over Safety

If a woman is attending a co-ed program, particularly a residential program or detoxification centre, it is important to ensure that women staff are available on every shift. It is also important to ensure that women have access to separate facilities to respect their right to privacy and safety.

Gender of the Counsellor

Some women — especially women who have been abused by men — may prefer their counsellor to be a woman. Similarly, some immigrant and refugee women might not feel comfortable with a male doctor due to their cultural or religious beliefs.

Agencies with a higher proportion of women on their treatment staff tend to attract a higher proportion of women to their programs.

You can help women by finding women counsellors and physicians in your area who are knowledgeable about substance use problems. You can also find out the proportion of women staff at treatment programs and whether a woman can be assured that she will have a woman counsellor.

Helping Treatment Reflect the Needs of Women

Alcohol and other drug treatment programs and services can be made more relevant for women in various ways. In general, women-sensitive treatment programs are those that:

- consider women's specific treatment needs
- reduce barriers for women getting treatment and recovering from their problematic use of substances
- take place in a safe environment and in a context that reflects women's ways of thinking and interacting
- recognize women's socialization, roles and status within society
- have counsellors who have recognized and dealt with their own attitudes towards women who have alcohol or other drug problems

But even women-sensitive programs may not meet the needs of all women. For example, women from diverse cultural backgrounds may find it difficult to have all their needs met in culturally-appropriate ways. They may have different spiritual needs, respond better to certain therapeutic approaches, or define "dependence on substances" in different ways.

The following is a checklist that you can use in deciding whether a program meets the needs of the woman you are referring.

WHAT IS WOMEN-SENSITIVE TREATMENT?

Women-sensitive or women-oriented treatment programs:

❏ offer a broad range of services (e.g., family and children's services, health services) in-house or in coordination with other programs

❏ take a holistic approach to a woman's treatment and recovery

❏ make the physical and emotional environment as comfortable and safe as possible (e.g., furniture, culture of the program, interactions between clients and staff)

❏ have women on staff as counsellors and in leadership positions

❏ have sexual harassment policies

❏ recognize that women's issues around substance use are different from men's

❏ recognize that women's treatment needs are different from men's

❏ recognize that women's treatment needs are not all the same

❏ educate women about substance use and its effects on their bodies, relationships, and coping skills

❏ understand the importance of relationships in women's lives

❏ empower women (e.g., increase self-esteem, develop coping skills, offer job training)

❏ stress wellness and ways that women can nurture themselves

❏ work together with women to plan goals for change

❏ offer women-only groups

❏ are sensitive to all women regardless of sexual orientation, culture, race, age, socioeconomic status, etc.

Program Philosophy and Requirements

Some programs are based on a disease/medical model of treatment while others may use a cognitive-behavioral, biopsychosocial or harm-reduction approach. It is important to know the philosophy and requirements of the treatment program to which you refer women since these may affect how specific issues are handled (e.g., relapse). For example, some programs (particularly residential programs) may require participants to leave if they drink or use other drugs while attending the program. [See *"Understanding Different Theoretical and Philosophical Orientations"* in Chapter 2 for a discussion of the various approaches.]

Some programs may have admission requirements such as being drug-free for a specific period before attending the program, not being on any type of mood-altering medication (including medications for major psychiatric disorders), and not having a co-occurring problem (e.g., mental health problem, legal charges pending).

Some programs require women to give urine samples for drug analysis. Sometimes the process of giving a sample is supervised. For some women, these requirements are offensive and intrusive, and represent a barrier to trust and commitment to the program. If urine screening is part of the treatment program, it is important that program staff ensure that the client fully understands the reasons for screening, and that staff are sensitive to difficulties that a woman may have, and be willing to explore alternatives when the need arises.

While attending a program, participants may be required to attend certain types of activities (e.g., AA meetings, religious services, group therapy).

It is important that you and the woman you are referring are familiar with the program philosophy and requirements to ensure a match with the woman's needs and also to avoid any unpleasant surprises while she attends the program.

Sexual Orientation

Some programs, particularly women-only programs, have developed support groups for lesbians and provide an overall environment that is lesbian-positive. In some communities, Alcoholics Anonymous (AA) has special groups for gays, lesbians and bisexuals, or local support services or groups may be available through the gay/lesbian community. You need to be aware of which options are available for lesbian and bisexual women, what their limitations may be, what concerns or fears a woman may have about attending a program, and where she can get additional support around issues of sexual orientation and lifestyle.

What Does the Program Offer Women Clients?

Treatment programs have traditionally been designed by men and for men. The language used, style of counselling and issues discussed in these programs are those that typify men's lives. When women and men are treated together in groups, the following dynamics tend to occur:

- men's use of language and the way in which they interact (with each other, with women) sets the tone — men tend to do most of the talking and also tend to interrupt when someone else is speaking
- women tend to take on a nurturing role with the men in the group
- women's unique issues are usually not addressed
- sexual tension and relationships develop between some women and men

There are times when mixed-gender groups may be the best option for women:

- some women prefer to receive treatment in groups that also include men
- appropriate women-only groups may not be available or easily accessible
- with the support of a well-trained counsellor and the other group members, women can address issues that arise with men in treatment, thus empowering them to deal with situations in their own lives

Mixed-gender groups can be made more suitable for women in the following ways:

- have a number of women as counsellors and in leadership roles — this will provide women with strong role models and help to ensure that programming better reflects women's styles and needs
- work to neutralize gender-related assumptions, biases and behaviors (your own and clients') — eliminate sexist language, encourage equal participation from all group members, etc.
- try to ensure that men do not outnumber women in the group and never have only one woman in a group of men
- ensure that a woman is co-group leader — mixed groups should not be co-facilitated by two counsellors of the same gender

BENEFITS OF WOMEN-ONLY GROUPS

❑ Women have issues that they feel more comfortable discussing without men present. These issues include:

- how women's bodies work and how they are affected by alcohol and other drugs
- factors relating to women's reproductive systems (PMS, pregnancy, menopause)
- eating issues (which are most common in women)
- violence against women (which is usually done by men)
- feelings about her ability to be a good mother
- sexuality and sexual behavior while drinking or using drugs

❑ Women understand each other better and can share similar experiences.

❑ It is easier to eliminate sexist language.

❑ Women tend to speak differently than men — women are more likely to try to connect rather than compete with one another.

❑ Women can give each other more physical support by touching or holding one another.

❑ Women learn to value themselves and other women and can provide role models for one another.

❑ Women are not treated as sexual objects.

❑ Women are more likely to talk about and focus on their own problems instead of trying to take care of or please the men in the group.

❑ Women can learn to be more assertive.

COUNSELLING ISSUES

Problems with substance use often go hand in hand with other major issues in women's lives — physical and sexual violence, eating issues, issues around sexuality, depression and self-harming behaviors (e.g., slashing skin, attempting suicide). While it is not always clear which came first — the substance use or other problems — each issue must be addressed during treatment as well as afterwards as part of continuing care (e.g., in aftercare groups).

A woman who is coming for substance use treatment may not recognize or want to talk about other sensitive areas of her life. Asking about these issues in a natural, non-judgmental way should increase the likelihood of her being able to openly acknowledge her experiences, feelings and concerns. It is important that a counsellor support a woman in addressing the issues that she is prepared (or not prepared) to deal with in whatever depth she feels ready to at any time.

If you plan to refer a woman to a specialized substance use treatment program, it is important to find out if the program includes counselling for her co-existing problems or if she will at least get support in finding an appropriate counsellor or program that will address these issues.

If you and the client decide that she will continue to see you for one of her co-existing problems but you do not feel you have the skills to address the other co-existing problem(s), you and the client may agree that she should be referred to someone else for help with that issue. You will then need to work out a referral plan and ensure that you all agree on the woman's goals for change. In working out this arrangement, consider the following questions: Does the other counsellor or program have a similar approach to alcohol and other drug problems? Does the counsellor feel comfortable working with a woman on a co-existing issue at the same time that she is working on her problem with substances? How does the program view and handle relapse? Does it have a similar approach to working with women?

Coping with Anger

Women may be experiencing, recognizing and coping with their anger without the use of substances for the first time in their lives.

- a woman may need help in understanding why she is angry and will need to learn how to express her anger in an assertive manner (i.e., not a passive or an overly aggressive manner)
- this expression of feelings should be viewed as a positive step that will enhance a woman's self-concept and assertiveness skills

51.

- asserting her true feelings in this way benefits the woman and decreases the likelihood that she will use alcohol and other drugs to cope

Coping with Guilt and Shame

Women in recovery often experience enormous guilt and shame. Although they need to reflect on their behavior, they need to do so in a way that does not blame them and make them feel guilty.

- some issues in a woman's life may be beyond her control — she should not be held accountable for everything that happens in her life
- in areas where she can make real changes, a woman needs to be supported in her efforts instead of being confronted with her failures

Recovering women with children feel especially guilty about the effect that their substance use and parenting style has had on their children.

- a recovering woman needs to believe that she can be a good mother — she may need parenting training to develop the necessary skills
- women need time to resolve their guilt feelings — they need to acknowledge how their past substance use has affected their children (possibly during pregnancy as well as afterwards) but they also need to see the changes they have made and move on in a positive direction

Coping with Physical and Sexual Violence

Many, if not most, women with substance use problems have experienced physical and/or sexual violence (including sexual assault) at some time in their lives. In fact, they may be in a violent relationship now.

Women who have experienced this type of violence commonly feel fear, anxiety, depression, anger, shame, lowered self-esteem, powerlessness and helplessness. It is important to deal with these feelings as well as with the underlying violence and co-occurring substance use.

If a woman tells you that she has experienced violence, it is important for her to know that you believe her, that it was not her fault, and that help is available. Coping with the experience of violence (e.g., memories, feelings) may put a woman at higher risk of relapse. Thus it must become part of her treatment program and not used as an excuse to ask her to leave treatment. [Refer to *The Courage to Heal* by Ellen Bass and Laura Davis.]

It is critical to consider a woman's safety. She may be at risk for self-harming behaviors (e.g., slashing or burning herself, suicide) and/or may be at risk of violence in a current relationship.

A woman who is living in a violent relationship or situation may need to develop the confidence and skills to protect herself. For example, she may need a safe place to go to (such as a woman's shelter or a residential treatment program) and a plan for how to get there.

Women in treatment may be acting violently toward their children. If they are, it is important to ensure that the children are safe. As a counsellor, you have a legal obligation to report this situation to the appropriate child welfare agency. Do this with the woman's knowledge and, hopefully, with her approval.

A word about stopping drug use: When people stop their regular use of alcohol or other drugs, we often expect them to feel better — but at first they may in fact feel worse. For example, for women who have experienced physical and/or sexual violence, their emotions often come flowing back, they may have flashbacks, or they may not be able to recognize what it is that they are feeling. At times like that, women may use substances again for a while or they may experience a more serious relapse.

When working with women who experience flashbacks, it is important for you to become knowledgeable about these issues. One good source is Trauma and Recovery *by Judith Herman.*

Developing Appropriate Coping Skills

Women who are learning to cope without the use of alcohol or other drugs need to develop a variety of positive coping skills, which can include the following:
- personal goal setting
- financial planning
- parenting training
- how to communicate with and relate to others

53.

- developing a support system (e.g., family and friends, self-help groups, for child care)
- assertiveness training
- setting boundaries
- stress and crisis management
- how to manage their lives when they are no longer in a treatment program
- grounding techniques
- understanding self-esteem
- exploring their rights
- violence against women and its link with substance use
- grief and loss
- relationships and trust
- recreation and leisure

Eating Issues

A woman may report craving certain foods and find it difficult not to eat them — in the same way that she reports craving for and use of alcohol or other drugs. In such a case, a woman may be using food for comfort and may need to develop coping strategies around these foods — just like with alcohol and other drugs.

Food is a necessity of life. A woman with anorexia, bulimia, or compulsive overeating or undereating habits needs guidance in establishing a normal, healthy diet. To do this, she needs to:

- understand why she eats the way she does — her issues around eating may have begun as an attempt to lose weight, as a means of controlling some aspect of her life, or in response to some other social or emotional need
- learn to distinguish between eating due to hunger, boredom, anxiety or habit
- change her relationship with food and eating — she needs to stop dieting and start eating normally
- appreciate and accept her body's own healthy weight and shape — it will be helpful for her to understand that there is no normal (or ideal) body weight or shape
- find pleasure and comfort in activities other than eating

An eating problem can be life-threatening and in some cases you and the client may need to consider referral to a specialized clinic.

Financial, Legal and Job Assistance

Women entering treatment may have financial, legal and work-related issues that need to be resolved.

Finances

Women may not have enough money to enter treatment and may need financial help with child care arrangements, living arrange-ments or other rental costs, transportation costs, and loss of income.

Consult with provincial or municipal social services depart-ments and family and children's services to determine what finan-cial support women can obtain. Also provide women with a range of treatment options so that they can choose one that costs less.

Legal Issues

Women may have legal issues to deal with before entering treat-ment or while they are in treatment. They may need time away from the program to make court appearances, for example, or they may need ongoing support in dealing with the legal system. Some com-mon legal issues for women with substance use problems include child custody issues, separation or divorce proceedings, harassment or stalking by a violent partner or ex-partner, and outstanding charges for a variety of offences (e.g., driving while impaired, drug possession or trafficking, shoplifting).

Some substance treatment programs are reluctant to accept clients with outstanding charges against them or clients who are involuntary referrals (i.e., forced by a court decision to get treat-ment). Or they may have rules about absences from the program to see a lawyer or attend court. Ensure that a woman knows what to expect when she starts a program and that the program staff are aware that she may need to be absent to see a lawyer or attend court.

A counsellor and a woman who is involved with a legal or child welfare agency need to be clear about the counsellor's legal oblig-ations, the limits of confidentiality, the role of client consent, and issues of continued use of substances. A counsellor could be asked to provide information about a client's use of substances or progress in treatment by a child welfare agency or by a probation or parole officer. It is important to discuss these issues with a woman so that her safety can be maintained while the counsellor also fulfils her legal obligations. [See Appendix at the end of this section for a more detailed discussion of these issues.]

Employment Issues

Women may need help around work-related issues, particularly during the continuing-care stage of treatment. They may need help in arranging time off work to get treatment, upgrading their skills or education, finding a job, changing jobs, and dealing with harassment or other work-related problems. This may involve referring them to adult education programs, upgrading or retraining programs, or vocational counselling services. It may also be important to ensure that a woman has continuing support at her workplace through an employee assistance counsellor or an occupational health nurse, if available.

Health Issues

Health Care

Health care is an important part of any treatment program. For women this is especially true since women develop serious substance use-related health problems faster than men do.

If a particular treatment site does not provide medical services, you may have to help a woman find a physician for routine medical care.

Physical and mental health needs of women include standard medical services, such as:

- an annual physical examination (including a Pap smear)
- diagnosis and treatment of unhealthy physical and mental conditions
- information on safer sex practices
- birth control and family planning information, if relevant
- pregnancy testing and pre- and post-natal care
- health promotion advice (e.g., nutrition, fitness, how to assert herself with health care providers)
- sleep patterns

Other health care models can be used together with standard medical care. These include chiropractic, massage therapy, naturopathy and acupuncture. These services, however, are not usually covered by provincial health care plans.

Sexually-Transmitted Infections (STIs)

Women with substance use problems are at higher risk of getting sexually-transmitted infections, such as Hepatitis B, Hepatitis C and HIV (leading to AIDS). This is especially true if they or their partners are injection drug users, have multiple sex partners, and/or exchange sex for drugs.

- all drugs, but especially alcohol, suppress the body's immune system and make a person more prone to infection
- during intercourse, the person receiving fluids into the body is the person most at risk for getting an infection from the other person
- an individual's reasoning and decision-making skills around having sex are impaired when using substances; for example, a substance-using woman may have sex with someone she would not otherwise get involved with or she may have unprotected sex (i.e., not use a condom)
- a woman with a substance use problem is more likely than other women to be in a violent relationship where she is afraid to assert herself and set limits (such as insisting on safer sex practices); she may be forced to have sex with many partners, to have sex without a condom, or to share used needles
- with women who are prostitutes, a man may negotiate the non-use of condoms by offering her more money — and if the woman has a substance use problem, getting money to buy more drugs becomes a priority for her

Women need reliable and accessible information about how to protect themselves from getting HIV infection and other sexually transmitted infections. Supporting women to take the following steps is most likely to reduce their risk of infection:

- safer use of alcohol and other drugs
- using safer sex practices (e.g., condom, dental dam)
- avoiding unprotected sex (even with a regular partner), multiple partners or partners who are injection drug users

- knowing where to obtain clean needles, learning how to clean needles (with bleach and water), and not sharing needles with anyone (including partners and family members) when injecting drugs

Provide women with information on resources (e.g., public health departments, STI clinics) that will give information on safer sex practices, how and where to obtain clean needles, and how to clean injection drug equipment.

Having AIDS or being HIV-positive brings a host of other problems that the counsellor and the woman need to face together.
- a woman has to decide whether she wants people to know she has AIDS or is HIV-positive because some people will discriminate against her when she seeks housing, work or access to other resources
- if a woman discloses her health status, her counsellor may need to advocate for services on her behalf
- she may have to cope with her own possible death and that of other family members and friends if they are also infected

Provide support for a woman to reduce or stop using alcohol or other drugs and ensure that counsellors you refer a woman to are knowledgeable about HIV and AIDS and provide a non-discriminatory atmosphere.

A number of publications address the issue of the HIV-positive client and treatment for substance use. For example, you could obtain the publication, *The H.I.V. Positive Client: A Guide for Addictions Treatment Professionals* by Michael McCrimmon and Kate Tschakovsky, Addiction Research Foundation. Or you could contact your provincial addictions agency or Ministry of Health for publications or guidelines on these issues.

Mental Health Issues

Women with substance use problems may also have an accompanying mental health problem. Common problems include depression, anxiety, agoraphobia (the fear of going outside and being in public spaces) and post-traumatic stress disorder. Multiple personality disorder sometimes occurs in women dealing with severe trauma from physical and/or sexual violence.

It is important to determine whether substances are being used to "medicate" mental health problems because eliminating a woman's substance use may allow her feelings to surface and put her at risk of relapsing. Exploring with a woman when she started to use substances heavily and which feelings or emotions trigger her substance use may help to determine this.

The effects of some substances may mimic mental health problems. Ideally, it is important that a woman be completely withdrawn from all substances before a mental health problem can be accurately assessed and a decision made about whether she requires medication. For example, long-term heavy alcohol use can look like depression and some illegal drugs can produce behaviors similar to a psychosis (e.g., seeing and hearing things that are not there).

Try to establish a good working relationship with a psychiatrist who is knowledgeable about alcohol and other drug problems or with a mental health clinic where staff have experience with co-occurring problems.

Relapse Prevention

Many people will have one or more episodes of using alcohol or other drugs at problem levels after a period of abstinence or reduced use. This is a normal part of the recovery process that involves making significant life changes and learning new skills. A one-time episode of such problem substance use is usually called a "lapse" while a more serious or longer episode of problem substance use is usually labelled a "relapse."

A lapse or relapse can occur for various reasons. Having a relapse, however, does not necessarily mean that a woman needs to go back into treatment. It may mean that she needs to do more work on her strategies to prevent relapse or that she needs help in addressing a current or past issue (e.g., trauma) in her life.

A woman who is unable to maintain her goals for reduced drinking may need to consider abstinence as her goal. And a woman who is having difficulty maintaining abstinence (i.e., she is having repeated or continuous relapses) may need to consider getting additional treatment or more intense treatment.

To help prevent a relapse, women need to develop knowledge, confidence and skills related to their substance use.

Knowledge includes:
- understanding under what conditions and in which situations people are most likely to drink or take drugs, such as:
    - experiencing unpleasant emotions (e.g., anger, sadness, anxiety)
    - physical discomfort (e.g., premenstrual tension, pain)
    - feeling the urge to drink or take other drugs (e.g., cravings, dreaming about using substances, dry drunk)
    - being in conflict with other people (e.g., getting into arguments, fights)
    - testing personal control (e.g., going to a bar, being with old friends who are heavy drinkers or drug users)
    - feeling social pressure to drink or use other drugs (e.g., at a party or social occasion, with a partner who drinks or uses drugs)
    - experiencing pleasant emotions (e.g., rewarding herself by using substances)
    - when experiencing pleasant times with other people (e.g., situations where drinking or drug use is expected, such as at weddings, religious celebrations, parties)
- what physical and emotional feelings to expect in the first few days, first few weeks or first few months after she stops using substances (so that experiencing uncomfortable physical and emotional feelings does not become a reason to start using alcohol or other drugs again)
- understanding her own pattern of substance use and what triggers her use (e.g., which days of the week she uses substances, at what times of day, under what circumstances, high-risk situations for substance use, and situations in which she feels more confident about not using substances)
- determining which coping strategies she can use for high-risk situations, which coping strategies have worked in the past or which ones she believes will work now)

Confidence and **Skills** include:
- practising her coping strategies — starting with situations in which she feels at low risk for using substances and gradually working up to high-risk situations
- becoming aware of her strengths, social supports and successful coping strategies
- being able to anticipate difficult situations and plan how to cope with them
- building a support network and an "emergency plan" if things are not going well, and learning how to use the plan (e.g., calling people when she feels well and also when she needs support)

A variety of program models and tools are available to help people identify high-risk situations for drinking or drug use and develop strategies to deal with them. *The Inventory of Drinking Situations (IDS-100)* and the *Situational Confidence Questionnaire (SCQ-39)* are both available from the Addiction Research Foundation.

Relationship Issues in Treatment

Women generally feel more concerned about and responsible for relationships than men. Consequently, involving a broader range of people — children, partner, parents, friends — in a woman's treatment program often increases her ability to make desired changes in her life.

Who Is a Woman's Family and Social Support Network?

"Family" may include any number of living arrangements or relationships. Let the client tell you whom she considers to be "family." She might describe:
- the so-called traditional family unit of husband, children and extended relations
- a lesbian relationship with friends as extended "family"
- being a single parent
- a "blended" family
- her family of origin

- a common-law partnership
- housemates
- people in her neighborhood

No matter how a woman defines her "family," she needs to know that her counsellor supports her lifestyle in a non-judgmental way.

An Important Note: Lesbians and bisexual women may have told some "family" members about their sexual orientation while keeping it a secret from others. Each woman's particular needs around confidentiality in this area will have to be respected.

Family Substance Use Problems

Involving a woman's family or social support network in her treatment program may not be easy or appropriate if the family member or friend also has a substance use problem. For instance:

- there may be substance use problems among members of a woman's family of origin, such as her father, mother or sibling(s)
- a woman's partner or close friend may have problems with substance use
- a woman's children may have alcohol- or drug-related birth effects and are likely to be affected by having a parent with substance use problems
- a woman's children may also be using substances
- a woman's children may be having other types of behavior problems

In some cases, family and friends may directly or indirectly support a woman's use of alcohol or other drugs. For example, they may deny she has a substance use problem because it may be inconvenient for them if she goes for treatment, they may be using substances themselves, or they may fear that eliminating her dependence on substances will change who she is and how she interacts with them.

Taking Responsibility for Relationships

Women have been labelled as "codependent" because they tend to work around a partner's behavior to make the relationship function. Codependence has become a negative label that blames women for behaviors they have developed to try to keep the relationship intact. This label has been used particularly for women living with a partner or with a child who has a substance use problem. In such a relationship, women often have to take on more of the roles and responsibilities because the partner is no longer fulfilling them. Sometimes in a relationship with a child with a substance use problem, a woman may want to "overprotect" her child.

A better concept is to remove the blame from women by helping them recognize that they have been socialized to please and take care of others and to bear the major responsibility for how relationships work.

Social Isolation

Women with substance use problems may become isolated and disconnected from significant people in their lives. Yet having healthy relationships is especially important to women and is central to their sense of worth and personal growth.

Developing Relationship Skills

It is important to try to work with a woman and the significant people in her life to create a balance in their relationships. Women need to care as much about themselves as they do about their relationships — yet they should not be shamed or criticized for being overly empathetic, nurturing and other-centred. These are positive qualities that simply need to be balanced by a similar concern for themselves.

Women in recovery need to find a healthy balance between independence and interdependence with others. They may need help in learning how to:
- create the proper balance between give and take in relationships
- feel more comfortable with their parenting skills
- develop a broad range of relationships with family, friends, spiritual groups, agencies, etc.

Involving a woman's partner in her substance use treatment (if relevant and appropriate for her) can help her look at the dynamics of

63.

the relationship and try to achieve a good balance between independence for herself and interdependence with her partner.

Involving family and friends in a woman's treatment can help them learn how to:
- be supportive of her desire to change and not reinforce her use of substances
- be aware that she may have changed in ways that they may find difficult to accept (e.g., increased assertiveness)
- deal with problems in their own lives that may relate to her substance use
- interact with her in ways that will enhance her self-esteem and her ability to assert herself
- deal with changes in their own lives when she decreases or stops her substance use
- possibly recognize their own substance use problems and be referred for counselling or treatment

Women's support groups, self-help programs, parent education/ support groups, and parent/child drop-in centres often help with these issues.

Parenting Issues
The issue of parenting and being a good mother is central to many women's identity. It can also be the cause of anxiety and guilt. This is especially true for women with substance use problems who have low self-esteem and who recognize that their substance use hurts their children as well as themselves. Thus treatment programs that focus on women's issues around their children are more likely to attract and keep women with children in their programs.

Providing child care on-site or through some other appropriate arrangement will relieve the stress for women who have no one else to take care of their children and are concerned that their children will be taken away from them. For example, can the agency provide a supervised area where children can wait (e.g., with books and toys)?

Children may need certain services (e.g., assessment and referral, education, children's groups) as a result of growing up in a family with substance use problems. In particular, they may need some explanation and support about substance use and how their mothers' lives may have been affected, and what she is experiencing as she makes changes. Some children may believe that they are responsible for their parent's substance use problem and need to be reassured that it is not their fault.

Women whose children have developmental and/or other problems (e.g., alcohol-related birth effects) because of her drug use while pregnant may have special requirements and may need to be linked to specialized services.

Depending on the age of the children, they could be included in some discussion and education on substance use as part of a woman's counselling process.

The issue of a child's safety should be addressed. A woman may be in a relationship where her partner or another family member is abusing her children, or occasionally she may be abusing her children herself.

A substance-using woman may benefit from a parenting program that teaches her coping skills and shows her how to enhance her children's physical, mental and emotional health. Such a parenting program could teach a woman how to:

- give her children proper physical care
- stimulate her children by talking with them, reading to them, engaging them in physical activity, and exposing them to a variety of situations and environments
- create a safe and trusting environment
- enhance her children's confidence and self-esteem
- help her children develop healthy relationships with family and friends
- set limits and use appropriate discipline methods
- enhance her own confidence as a mother, develop an interest in her children's lives, and find joy in being with her children

Note: Family counselling services, child welfare services, women's support groups, self-help programs, parent education/support groups, and parent/child drop-in centres may also help with relationships and parenting issues.

Sexuality Issues

Women who stop using substances may experience sex without alcohol or other drugs for the first time in their lives. Any type of closeness or intimacy (especially sexual) may produce feelings of fear and anxiety if a woman has always relied on alcohol or other drugs in such situations. A woman will need to discover how her body and emotions respond sexually without substances. It may be helpful to encourage a woman to first start exploring her body without a partner.

The counselling situation can provide an opportunity to help a woman talk about her fears and help her deal with her feelings. A woman may also need information on issues such as:
- how her body works and what to expect when having sex without alcohol or other drugs
- reproductive issues and birth control
- how to give herself "permission" to engage in sexual activity or how to say "no" when she does not want to have sex
- how to have safer sex

Many women who have experienced physical or sexual violence use alcohol or other drugs to numb their feelings when having sex. They may have confused feelings about men and may need the opportunity to talk about the difference between the sexual act and love.

A woman may be questioning her sexual orientation or dealing with disclosure about her sexual orientation for the first time. Showing that you are not judgmental and that you accept her for who she is will help her deal with her identity issues in a positive way that does not lead to relapse.

Women and Self-Help

Many women with substance use problems respond best to minimal outside intervention. They find they can get better using their own initiative and getting help and support from people they trust.

Individual Self-Help

Women tend to be good at working out their problems on an informal basis by themselves or with the help of friends.

Women in the early stages of developing a problem with drinking or using other drugs may find that they can successfully use self-help methods to reduce or eliminate their substance use:

- several self-help books, tapes and programs are available
- women should choose a self-help program that is suited to their value system and that they think they are likely to stick with
- there are no structural barriers to engaging in a program of individual self-help — there are no geographical or child care restrictions; the cost is lower; it is good for the disabled, the elderly, and certain job routines; it is anonymous (thus eliminating the fear of being stigmatized); and a woman can be independent (i.e., she does not need a counsellor)

Women drinkers who successfully reduce or eliminate their alcohol use on their own report two main strategies that help them maintain that goal:

- they keep track of how much alcohol they buy and count their drinks
- they avoid what they perceive to be risky situations that might trigger their drinking (e.g., going to bars, being with heavy drinkers, being isolated or feeling alone, or being in a conflict situation)

A counsellor can provide support for a woman using a self-help program by:

- supporting a woman to ensure that using self-help methods does not isolate her and that she has a social support system in place
- supporting her to ensure that she is overcoming structural barriers such as lack of privacy, and access to materials she needs to work through the self-help program

In addition to self-help books on reducing alcohol use, other self-help books are available on issues that may be influencing women's alcohol and other drug use. As a counsellor, you could create a resource centre within your own work environment so that clients could have easy access to these resources. Or you could provide clients with a list of pamphlets, books, and other resources that you feel would be helpful.

Saying When: How to Quit Drinking or Cut Down by
Martha Sanchez-Craig is available from the Addiction
Research Foundation to assist women who are at an early
stage of developing a drinking problem. This type of self-
help material has been designed for people who have problems with drinking only. You could also contact your
provincial addictions agency or Ministry of Health regarding other materials available in your province.

Mutual-Aid Groups

Many mutual-aid groups are offered in communities across Canada.
Most are based on the 12-step model of Alcohol Anonymous (e.g.,
Narcotics Anonymous, Cocaine Anonymous, Alateen and Al-Anon for
family members). Alcoholics Anonymous (AA) was designed by men
for men yet many women are members today. Another mutual-aid model
is Women for Sobriety (WFS), which was founded by a woman for other
women. Women for Sobriety is not available everywhere, however,
while an AA group can be found in most communities. Both groups
were originally designed for people with problems with alcohol but the
same principles can also be applied to people having problems with other
drugs. Most 12-step groups focus on individual change without recognizing the need for political and social change as well. WFS, however, is
one organization that looks at the broader context of women's lives and
stresses the need for change in all aspects of women's lives.

Mutual-aid programs are usually one of the social supports
encouraged during and after a treatment program. There are many
benefits of mutual-aid groups such as:
- there are no professionals or authority figures
- people realize that they are not alone and they are not the only
  ones with problems
- they give people a sense of belonging to a caring community
- people share their experiences, feelings and coping skills
- meetings provide a social context that is alcohol- and drug-free

An Important Note: *Counsellors should alert women that some
people attending meetings may be still using substances and can
put other members at risk. Women should also be cautious about*

jumping into social relationships too quickly, exchanging phone numbers, etc. Mutual-aid groups are support groups; they are not therapy groups or a place to develop instant new relationships.

Introducing Women to Mutual-Aid Groups

Going into any new situation can be scary. Ask a woman if she would like to go with someone else for her first few meetings. AA can usually arrange this or a counsellor may develop contacts with other women members in a mutual aid group whom she can call on to take a woman to a meeting.

Become familiar with the local mutual-aid groups and attend some meetings so you can tell a woman what to expect when she goes to her first meeting. Also be aware of the different types of meetings that are available (e.g., open or closed meetings, all women's groups, groups for gays and lesbians).

If a women lives in a community where a variety of different groups meet on different days and in different locations (this is particularly true of groups like AA), she might like to try several different groups until she finds one that suits her best.

Some women may be reluctant to go to AA or a similar mutual aid group because they may be afraid of being labelled "alcoholic" or of seeing someone they know. For some women, going to a meeting presents real barriers in terms of transportation, child care and other family responsibilities. Explore with a woman any potential barriers or fears she may have about getting involved in a mutual-aid group and develop ways you can support her in overcoming them.

> For a more detailed description of mutual-aid programs, read *Many Roads, One Journey: Moving Beyond the 12 Steps* by Charlotte Davis Kasl.

ACCOUNTABILITY ISSUES

Various ethical and legal issues may arise when working with clients, such as issues around confidentiality, sexual harassment, discrimination, and relationships between staff members and clients. All organizations and agencies working with clients should develop guidelines around proper behavior and action to take when dealing with these issues.

Information given by a client to a counsellor should remain confidential unless the client indicates the information may be shared with certain people or under certain circumstances. Some situations, however, require the counsellor to report information received from the client, including the following: the client tells you that she intends to harm herself or someone else; you suspect child abuse; or the client's file is subpoenaed by a court of law. It is important to explain these limits to confidentiality to the client.

There are specific situations that may occur when working with women with alcohol or other drug problems. It is important to put in place policies and procedures to address such situations. Following are four common situations. The appendix at the end of this section contains the legal advice that ARF lawyers provided to assist ARF staff in developing policies and procedures to address such situations. You may wish to consider this advice in establishing your own agency policies and procedures.

Situation A: The client is intoxicated and the counsellor is aware that the client intends to leave the counsellor's office and drive home.

Situation B: The client gives the counsellor an illegal drug so the counsellor can dispose of it.

Situation C: The client tells the counsellor that she has been drinking or taking other drugs and the counsellor is aware that this is a breach of her probation order or a violation of her parole.

Situation D: The client is also a client of the Children's Aid Society. The counsellor is aware that the client is continuing to drink or use other drugs in a problematic way, but the Children's Aid Society is not aware of this information and is making custody decisions based on the client being substance-free.

70.

APPENDIX

Legal Advice on Accountability Issues

A. A Counsellor's Duty to Report the Intoxication of a Client

(i) Criminal

An ARF counsellor must be taken to know that operating a motor vehicle while impaired or while the concentration of alcohol in the blood exceeds the legal limits ("Over 80") contrary to the Criminal Code both constitute crimes.

There is, in general, no obligation upon any citizen to report to the police the crime, or potential crime, of anyone including a client. This principle applies to a counsellor at the ARF and his or her relationship with a client. This general principle can be modified by statute in which case the statutory provisions would determine the circumstances in which an obligation to report would exist. There is no such statutory provision, at this point in time, which would compel the counsellor to report a crime, or potential crime, to the police.

Notwithstanding the foregoing, a citizen who reports to the police a crime or potential crime is protected from legal liability to the person whom he or she so reported provided that in making the report the citizen did so without malice and in good faith. Thus, an ARF counsellor who did report to the police a client's intention to drive while impaired or drive while Over 80 would be protected from legal liability if he or she did so in good faith and without malice.

(ii) Civil Liability

A counsellor who is aware that the client is intoxicated and intends to drive home must, reasonably, also be taken to know that the client may cause personal injury to himself or herself and to others and, in addition, may cause property damage. The question, then, is whether or not the counsellor owes a duty to the client and/or to third parties to take steps to prevent the client from driving while intoxicated and, if so, what steps.

In our view, it is possible that a court would hold that the counsellor, and therefore the ARF, owed a duty to the client and/or to

71.

third parties to warn the client of the risks inherent of driving while intoxicated and to suggest to the client alternatives to driving while intoxicated such as public transit, calling, or having the counsellor call, a family member to pick up the client, taking a taxi or simply waiting until able to drive or, failing to so persuade the client, by threatening, if necessary, to call the police. The existence of the possibility of such a duty being found to rest upon the ARF counsellor compels him or her to take the foregoing steps in order to protect against possible civil liability. It is not, however, necessary nor advisable for the counsellor to seek to physically restrain the client or remove his or her keys.

A counsellor who takes these steps of warning the client of the risks of driving while intoxicated and suggesting alternatives should carefully record, in writing, the particulars of such steps.

The foregoing presumes, of course, that the ARF did not provide the intoxicants to the client.

B. Disposal of Illegal Drugs

A number of statutes make the possession of certain substances illegal. There is, however, authority for the proposition that possession purely for the purposes of disposal does not constitute illegal possession of that substance. Accordingly, if the client were to give such a substance to an ARF counsellor and the counsellor received the substance for the purpose of disposal, no crime would be committed. It would be imperative, however, that the substance be disposed of immediately. An accurate record should be kept of the identity of the person from whom the substance was received, the identity of the person who received the substance, what the substance was alleged to be, the approximate quantity of the substance (in the absence of any other way of measuring quantity), the time of receipt of the substance and the time of disposal.

There is no obligation upon the ARF counsellor to report to the police or any other authority the delivery of the illegal substance for the purpose of disposal.

C. Breach of Parole or Probation

The relationship between a counsellor and the client does not create an obligation to report to either a probation or parole offi- .

cer a breach by the client of the terms of either his or her probation or parole.

It is quite possible that during the term of probation or parole, a
probation officer or a parole officer might contact the counsellor and
ask the counsellor if, to his or her knowledge, there had been a breach
by the client of the terms of parole or probation. Should such a cir-
cumstance arise, we are of the view that the counsellor ought to advise
the probation or parole officer, as the case may be, that the information is confidential and cannot be disclosed save by due process.

The more difficult question would be what obligation would
rest on the counsellor in the event, quite unlikely in practice, that
probation or parole were granted on the express understanding that
the client would attend counselling and, further, that the counsellor
had created some sort of direct relationship with the probation or
parole, that any breach of probation or parole be reported by the
counsellor to the appropriate authorities and all parties had agreed
to that arrangement, including the client, then the report can and
should be made.

D. Duty to Report to the Children's Aid Society

(i) Child in Need of Protection

Section 72(2) of the *Child and Family Services Act*, R.S.O. 1990, c.
C.11 (the "Act") provides:

> *A person who believes on reasonable grounds that a child is*
> *or may be in need of protection shall forthwith report the*
> *belief and information upon which it is based to a society.*

A "person" is not defined in the Act and, clearly, includes anyone. The term "society" is defined as an approved agency designated as the Children's Aid Society. The phrase "...in need of protection..." is broadly defined. A child is in need of protection, as
defined in Section 37 of the Act, where:

    (a) the child has suffered physical harm, inflicted by the person
        having charge of the child or caused by that person's failure
        to care and provide for or supervise and protect the child
        adequately;

(b) there is a substantial risk that the child will suffer physical harm inflicted or caused as described in clause (a);

(c) the child has been sexually molested or sexually exploited, by the person having charge of the child or by another person where the person having charge of the child knows or should know of the possibility of sexual molestation or sexual exploitation and fails to protect the child;

(d) there is substantial risk that the child will be sexually molested or sexually exploited as described in clause (c);

(e) the child requires medical treatment to cure, prevent or alleviate physical harm or suffering and the child's parent or the person having charge of the child does not provide, or refuses or is unavailable or unable to consent to, the treatment;

(f) the child has suffered emotional harm, demonstrated by severe
   (i)   anxiety;
   (ii) depression;
   (iii) withdrawal; or
   (iv) self-destructive or aggressive behaviour, and the child's parent or the person having charge of the child does not provide, or refuses or is unavailable or unable to consent to, services or treatment to remedy or alleviate the harm;

(g) there is substantial risk that the child will suffer emotional harm of the kind described in clause (f), and the child's parent or the person having charge of the child does not provide, or refuses or is unavailable or unable to consent to, services or treatment to prevent the harm;

(h) the child suffers from a mental, emotional or developmental condition that, if not remedied, could seriously impair the child's development and the parent or the person having charge of the child does not provide, or refuses or is unavailable or unable to consent to, treatment to remedy or alleviate the condition;

(i) the child has been abandoned, the child's parent has died or is unavailable to exercise his or her custodial rights over the child and has not made adequate provision for the child's care and custody, or the child is in a residential placement and the parent refuses or is unable or unwilling to resume the child's care and custody;

(j) the child is less than twelve years old and has killed or seriously injured another person or caused serious damage to another person's property, services or treatment are necessary to prevent a reoccurence and the child's parent or the person having charge of the child does not provide, or refuses or is unavailable or unable to consent to, those services or treatment;

(k) the child is less than twelve years old and has on more than one occasion injured another person or caused loss or damage to another person's property, with the encouragement of the person having charge of the child or because of that person's failure or inability to supervise the child adequately; or

(l) the child's parent is unable to care for the child and the child is brought before the court with the parent's consent and, where the child is twelve years of age or older, with the child's consent, to be dealt with under this Part.

The duty imposed by Section 72(2) of the Act is not a duty the breach of which gives rise to prosecution of the person who failed to report his or her belief that a child is or may be in need of protection.

(ii) Duty to Report Child Abuse

A child may be in need of protection because that child is likely to suffer abuse. It should be noted, however, that the circumstances that would or could give rise to a child being in need of protection are much broader than those circumstances in which a child may suffer abuse. In the latter instance, the Act has certain additional requirements of certain categories of persons.

Section 72(3) of the Act imposes a further duties on those who carry out certain professional or official duties. Among those professionals or officials are:

(a) health care professionals including but not limited to physicians, nurses, dentists, pharmacists and psychologists; and

(b) social workers and family counsellors.

Those professionals who, in the course of their professional or official duties, have reasonable grounds to suspect that a child is or may be suffering or may have suffered abuse shall forthwith report the suspicion and the information on which it is based to a society. The phrase "...to suffer abuse..." when used in reference to a child means to be in need of protection within the meaning of clauses 37(2)(a)(c)(e)(f) or (h) all of which have been set out above.

Failure of such a professional to comply with the statutory obligation of Section 72(3) of the Act can give rise to prosecution under the Act. Section 85 of the Act provides that a person of con-travention of subsection 72(3), has the obligation to report child abuse and that person and a director, officer or employee of the cor-poration that authorizes, permits or concurs in such a contravention by the corporation is guilty of an offence and on conviction is liable to a fine of not more than $1,000.00.

Accordingly, if the ARF counsellor is of the view that the client's continued drinking and drug use are such as to give rise to a child of the client or child with whom the client is in contact being in need of protection, that counsellor is obliged to so report to the Society.

Like provisions to those in the Act exist in all the other Canadian provinces and territories. Below is a chart setting out the comparable, although it should be noted not identical, statutory provisions in other jurisdictions. Those in other jurisdictions should be quite careful to ensure that they follow the specific statutory provision applicable in that jurisdiction.

Finally, it should also be made clear that any ARF counsellor with reasonable grounds to suspect that a child is or may be suf-fering or may have suffered from abuse is obliged, before report-ing such abuse, to comply with internal ARF protocol on child-abuse reporting.

PROVINCE	ACT	REPORT ABUSE TO:
Alberta	*Child Welfare Act,* chap. C-8.1	Director
British Columbia	*Family and Child Services Act,*. S.B. Chap. 11, Index Chap. 119.1 s. 7	Superintendent (in effect this this is delegated to social worker) *Jan. 1, 1996 this Act is being repealed and replaced by a new Act, s. 14 The duty to report will be to the Director of person designated by the Director.
Manitoba	*Child and Family Services Act,* R.S.M. c.8, s. 18.	Agency, Parent or Guardian of the Child
New Brunswick	*Family Services Act,* R.S.N.B. S.N. 1992, c. F-2.2, s.30.	Minister of Social Services
Newfoundland	*Child Welfare Act,* c.57 s. 1.	Director, Social Worker or Peace Officer
Northwest Territories	*Child Welfare Act,* R.S. NWT. 1988, c. C.6, s. 30 and 30.1	Superintendent
Nova Scotia	*Children and Family Services Act,* S.N.S. 1990, c.5, ss. 23-24.	An Agency
Ontario	*Child and Family Services Act,* R.S.O. 1990, c. C.11, s. 72.	Society (approved agency designated as Children's Aid Society)

PROVINCE	ACT	REPORT ABUSE TO:
Prince Edward Island	*Family and Child Services Act,* R.S. PEI 1988, c. F.2, s. 14.	Director of Peace Officer who shall report it to the Director
Quebec	*Youth Protection Act,* R.S.Q., P-34.1, s. 39.	Director Commission de Protection des Droits de la Jeunesse
Saskatchewan	*Child and Family Services Act,* R.S.S. s. 12.	An Officer or Peace Officer
Yukon	*Children's Act,* S.Y. 1986. c.22, s. 115. Education Act, S.Y. 1989-90, s. 168 (n) (Teachers' duty to report) *Child Care Act,* S.Y. ,1989-90 c.24, s. 38 (Childcare worker's duty to report)	Director, an Agent of the Director, or a Peace Officer Director, an Agent of the Director, or a Peace Officer

THE TWELVE STEPS OF ALCOHOLICS ANONYMOUS

1. We admitted we were powerless over alcohol — that our lives had become unmanageable.

2. Came to believe that a Power greater than ourselves could restore us to sanity.

3. Made a decision to turn our will and our lives over to the care of God *as we understood Him.*

4. Made a searching and fearless moral inventory of ourselves.

5. Admitted to God, to ourselves and to another human being the exact nature of our wrongs.

6. Were entirely ready to have God remove all these defects of character.

7. Humbly asked Him to remove our shortcomings.

8. Made a list of all persons we had harmed, and became willing to make amends to them all.

9. Made direct amends to such people wherever possible, except when to do so would injure them or others.

10. Continued to take personal inventory and when we were wrong promptly admitted it.

11. Sought through prayer and meditation to improve our conscious contact with God, *as we understood Him,* praying only for knowledge of His will for us and the power to carry that out.

12. Having had a spiritual awakening as the result of these steps, we tried to carry this message to alcoholics, and to practice these principles in all our affairs.

FEMINIST MODEL: TWELVE STEPS

1. Admitted we have a problem and recognized that our social environment contributes to our problem.

2. Recognized that help is available and that there are other ways of coping.

3. Became willing to change and asked for help.

4. Looked at both our healthy and unhealthy behaviors and coping skills.

5. Broke the silence — shared our lives, our pain, and our joy with others.

6. Became teachable; became willing to learn new healthy behaviors to replace our unhealthy behaviors.

7. Began to forgive ourselves and others.

8. Accepted responsibility for the harm we caused ourselves and others, recognizing that we do not need to take responsibility for those who harmed us.

9. Did what we could, without harming ourselves or others, to repair these damages and not repeat the unhealthy behavior.

10. Took responsibility for our day to day behavior, recognizing both our healthy and unhealthy behaviors.

11. Developed our individual spirituality, seeking inner wisdom and strength.

12. As a result of on-going healing and growth, we tried to live happier, healthier lives; learning to love and accept ourselves as we are.

© Sheri McConnell, from *Each Small Step: Breaking the Chains of Abuse and Addiction* edited by Marilyn MacKinnon. Used with the kind permission of the publisher, gynergy books, PO Box 2023, Charlottetown, P.E.I. C1A 7N7 Canada.

WOMEN FOR SOBRIETY (WFS)

New Life Program

1. I have a drinking problem that once had me.

2. Negative emotions destroy only myself.

3. Happiness is a habit I will develop.

4. Problems bother me only to the degree I permit them to.

5. I am what I think.

6. Life can be ordinary or it can be great.

7. Love can change the course of my world.

8. The fundamental object of life is emotional and spiritual growth.

9. The past is gone forever.

10. All love given returns two-fold.

11. Enthusiasm is my daily exercise.

12. I am a competent woman and have much to give life.

13. I am responsible for myself and my actions.

Source: Kirkpatrick. (1989).

REFERENCES

Abbott, Beverley A. (1990). *Women and Substance Abuse: Current Knowledge and Treatment Implications*. A Review of the Literature. 29.

Addiction Research Foundation. (1995). *LINK — Violence Against Women and Children in Relationships and the Use of Alcohol and Drugs: Searching for Solutions*. An Educational Package. Toronto: Addiction Research Foundation.

Alcoholics Anonymous World Services, Inc. *Alcoholics Anonymous (AA)*.

Annis, Helen M. & Davis, Christine S. (1991). Relapse Prevention. *Alcohol Health & Research World*, 15(3):204-212.

Beckman, Linda J. (1994). Treatment Needs of Women with Alcohol Problems. *Alcohol Health & Research World*, 18(3):206-211.

Blume, Sheila B. (1994). Women and Addictive Disorders. *American Society of Addiction Medicine*. 1-16.

Blume, Sheila B. (1992). Alcohol and other drug problems in women. In Lowinson, Joyce H., Ruiz, Pedro, Millman, Robert B. & Langrod, John G. (eds.). *Substance Abuse: A Comprehensive Textbook*. Baltimore: Williams & Wilkins, 794-807.

Boehnert, Joanna B. (1988). The psychology of women. In Burt, Sandra, Code, Lorraine & Dorney, Lindsay (eds.). *Changing Patterns: Women in Canada*. Toronto: McClelland and Stewart, 264-289.

Canadian Centre on Substance Abuse. (No Date). *Self-Help and Substance Abuse*. Self-Help Canada Series.

Center for Substance Abuse Prevention. (1993). Parenting Skills Training: Why So Important? *Healthy Delivery*, 1(3):6.

Center for Substance Abuse Treatment. (1994). *Practical Approaches in the Treatment of Women who Abuse Alcohol and Other Drugs*. Rockville, MD: U.S. Department of Health and Human Services, 275.

Covington, Stephanie S. (1991). Sororities of helping and healing: Women and mutual help groups. In Roth, Paula (ed.). *Alcohol and Drugs are Women's Issues*. Volume One: A Review of the Issues. Metuchen, NJ: Women's Action Alliance and Scarecrow Press, 85-92.

Finkelstein, Norma, Duncan, Sally Anne, Derman, Laura & Smeltz, Janet. (1990). *Getting Sober, Getting Well: A Treatment Guide for Caregivers who Work with Women*. Cambridge, MA: Women's Alcoholism Program of CASPAR, xiii, 632.

Ford, Peter M. & Kaufman, Hannah. (1993). AIDS and substance abuse. In Howard, Betty-Anne M., Harrison, Susan, Carver, Virginia & Lightfoot, Lynn (eds.). *Alcohol & Drug Problems: A Practical Guide for Counsellors.* Toronto: Addiction Research Foundation, 403-415.

Harris, Judith. (1992). Women's Detox and Treatment: New Challenges to Old Stereotypes. *Pathways,* (Sept/Oct):11-12.

Harrison, Susan. (1993). Working with women. In Howard, Betty-Anne M., Harrison, Susan, Carver, Virginia & Lightfoot, Lynn (eds.). *Alcohol & Drug Problems: A Practical Guide for Counsellors.* Toronto: Addiction Research Foundation, 195-218.

Health Canada. (1994). Family violence and substance abuse. *Information from The National Clearinghouse on Family Violence.* Ottawa: Health Canada, 10.

Howard, Betty-Anne M. & Hudson, Deborah. (1993). Sexuality, sexual problems, and sexual and physical assault. In Howard, Betty-Anne M., Harrison, Susan, Carver, Virginia & Lightfoot, Lynn (eds.). *Alcohol & Drug Problems: A Practical Guide for Counsellors.* Toronto: Addiction Research Foundation, 343-362.

Kaskutas, Lee Ann. (1994). What do women get out of self-help? Their reasons for attending. Women for Sobriety and Alcoholics Anonymous. *Journal of Substance Abuse Treatment,* 11(3):185-195.

Kasl, Charlotte Davis. (1992). *Many Roads, One Journey: Moving Beyond the 12 Steps.* New York: HarperCollins.

Kirkpatrick, Jean. (1989). *Women for Sobriety (WFS) New Life Program.* Quakertown, Pennsylvania.

Krestan, Jo-Ann & Bepko, Claudia. (1991). Codependency: The social reconstruction of female experience. In Bepko, Claudia (ed.). *Feminism and Addiction.* New York: Haworth Press, 49-66.

Levine, Helen. (1989). Feminist counselling: A woman-centred approach. In Carver, Virginia & Ponée, Charles (eds.). *Women, Work & Wellness.* Toronto: Addiction Research Foundation, 227-252.

McArthur, Lynne C. (1991). Women and AIDS. In Roth, Paula (ed.). *Alcohol and Drugs are Women's Issues.* Volume One: A Review of the Issues. Metuchen, NJ: Women's Action Alliance and Scarecrow Press, 114-119.

McConnell, Sheri. (1991). The Twelve Steps Modified. In MacKinnon, Marilyn (ed.). *Each Small Step: Breaking the Chains of Abuse and Addiction.* Charlottetown, PEI: gynergy, 144-146.

North Island Women's Services Society. (1984). *Working Together for Change: Women's Self-Help Handbook.*

Prather, Jane E. & Minkow, Nancy V. (1991). Prescription for despair: Women and psychotropic drugs. In Van Den Bergh, Nan (ed.). *Feminist Perspectives on Addiction.* New York: Springer, 87-99.

Reed, Beth Glover. (1987). Developing Women-Sensitive Drug Dependence Treatment Services: Why so difficult? *Journal of Psychoactive Drugs*, 19(2):151-164.

Reed, Beth Glover. (1985). Drug Misuse and Dependency in Women: The Meaning and Implications of Being Considered a Special Population or Minority Group. *The International Journal of the Addictions*, 20(1):13-62.

Sanchez-Craig, Martha. (1995). *Saying When: How to Quit Drinking or Cut Down.* Second Edition, Revised. Toronto: Addiction Research Foundation, ii, 82.

Schliebner, Connie T. (1994). Gender-Sensitive Therapy: An Alternative for Women in Substance Abuse Treatment. *Journal of Substance Abuse Treatment*, 11(6):511-515.

Smith, Vivian L. (1993). Exploring Gender Issues in Treatment. *Health Delivery*, 1(3):1-5.

Thom, Betsy. (1986). Sex Differences in Help-Seeking for Alcohol Problems — 1. The barriers to help-seeking. *British Journal of Addiction*, 81:777-788.

Underhill, Brenda L. (1991). Recovery needs of lesbian alcoholics in treatment. In Van Den Bergh, Nan (ed.). *Feminist Perspectives on Addiction.* New York: Springer, 73-86.

4

Screening, Identification, Assessment, Referral

ASKING ABOUT ALCOHOL AND OTHER DRUG USE

Understanding Your Biases and Stereotypes

Everyone has acquired various biases and stereotypes during their lives. As a counsellor it is especially important to:

- Be aware of your biases and stereotypes.
- Understand where your biases and stereotypes come from (societal and family attitudes). For example, you may have biases based on your own, or a family member's, experiences with alcohol or other drugs.
- Understand how your socialization affects the way you view other people and situations. Focus especially on areas where you are most likely to hold stereotypes about people and where the differences between you and the women you are working with may reinforce the counsellor-client power imbalance. These include issues around:
    - age
    - parenting abilities
    - ethnocultural background
    - physical appearance
    - socioeconomic status
    - lifestyle
    - educational level
    - sexual orientation

- physical and intellectual abilities
- sexuality
- experience with violence
- experience with drug use
- language and verbal abilities
- Recognize and try to set aside these attitudes when working with women who may be different from, and have different values than, yourself. Be especially careful about labelling or stereotyping women. If you find that these differences are affecting your ability to counsel effectively, seek support from your supervisor or peers.
- Respect and try to understand other people's ways of doing and saying things. For example, people from other cultures may use different verbal and nonverbal communication patterns. They may also define a substance use problem, what is helpful, and how and from whom they should seek help, differently than you.
- Use the same language the client uses, if appropriate.

If a woman feels you are making lifestyle judgments about her, this may:
- add to her low self-esteem
- contribute to her feelings of shame
- cause her to hold back information from you
- erode opportunities to build trust
- increase the chance that she will not come back or go on to get other support

As a counsellor, it is important to ask yourself more specific questions about situations you will face when working with women who have problems with substance use. In the following box on counsellor attitudes, can you answer "yes" in each situation?

86.

Could You Work Effectively (i.e., not impose your values) with a Woman who ...

❑ you feel is neglecting her child(ren)?

❑ has physically, sexually, emotionally or verbally abused her child(ren)?

❑ has given up her child(ren) or is expressing disinterest, hostility or not wanting them?

❑ drinks heavily and/or takes other drugs during pregnancy?

❑ you feel has totally inadequate parenting skills?

❑ has had or is thinking about having an abortion?

❑ wishes to end a marriage where there are school-aged children and where she seems to be well taken care of (i.e., financially)?

❑ has been married several times or has had many partners?

❑ insists on staying in a violent relationship?

❑ talks about the difficulties in her relationship with her female lover?

❑ spends most of her time with you in tears?

❑ makes a pass at you?

❑ is grieving the death of a child, partner or parent?

❑ has assaulted or killed someone?

❑ is just starting to "come out of the closet" (i.e., acknowledge she is a lesbian)?

❑ earns a living through prostitution?

❑ is beginning to have memories of childhood incest?

❑ talks of plans to commit suicide?

❑ is totally content being a homemaker?

❑ is often angry in interviews?

❑ is obese?

❑ is HIV-positive or has AIDS?

Source: Harrison. (1993).

Screening and Identification

WHY Should I Ask about Substance Use?

Drinking and other drug use is common in most cultures and is a normal part of many people's lifestyle.

Routinely asking about alcohol and other drug use gives a woman permission to talk about a topic that she may find difficult or may be embarrassed about.

Asking a woman about her alcohol or other drug use suggests that you think substance use is a normal part of everyday life. Displaying such an attitude makes it easier for women who may have a problem with substance use to talk about it. (It is important not just to ask women who you think show obvious signs of problem use or to make judgments about who you think may have a problem.)

The earlier a substance use problem is identified and addressed, the greater the chance of a successful outcome.

> ### WHY ASK THE QUESTIONS?
>
> Asking questions and providing feedback are therapeutic tools that:
>
> - identify problems
> - assess needs
> - give a holistic view of the woman
> - encourage self-analysis
> - build motivation
> - promote behavior change
> - provide an opening for health teaching

HOW Do I Ask about Substance Use?

You can ask questions about alcohol and other drug use in a number of ways. You can include substance use questions:

- as part of a routine intake or assessment
- as part of any initial or follow-up interview you have with a woman
- when talking with a woman about life issues and how she copes with them

Explain that questions about substance use are routine and that the client's responses are confidential.

Use language that both you and the client are comfortable with. For example, a woman may use slang or "street" names for drugs. If she uses names you do not understand, ask her what they mean.

Ensure that you and the client mean the same thing when you talk about substance use. For example, make sure you are both talking about the same quantity of alcohol when you refer to having a "drink."

Creating a Supportive Environment

Make sure the physical environment (e.g., your office) where you talk with the client is:
- comfortable
- safe
- private
- located with easy access to the door

Display information (posters and pamphlets) on alcohol and other drug use in your office.

Speak, ask questions and respond to the client in language that is:
- positive and caring — this will encourage the establishment of trust between you and the client
- direct
- non-judgmental — this will show that you accept the woman and what she is saying
- value-free and applies to all people and situations (e.g., ask about "important relationships" rather than marital status)
- respectful

Positively acknowledge the client's decision to seek help.

Explain why you are asking particular questions, why you need the information.

Ask questions that are:
- open-ended — these encourage the client to talk about herself, her life, and how she sees things
- neutral — ask the client what she sees as the positive and negative aspects of her alcohol or other drug use

Listen reflectively. Check with the client to ensure that you understand what she means — rather than assuming that you do. This involves:
- listening to the client
- hearing what the client says
- responding to the client — by making statements that indi-

89.

cate what you heard her say and checking with her to see if that is what she meant (i.e., not telling her what she meant)

Encourage the client to continue talking about and exploring her concerns, issues and feelings around her alcohol and other drug use. Ask her to:
- explain in which circumstances she feels the way she does or if is concerned about a particular issue
- give specific examples

Focus on a woman's strengths, on what has helped her make changes in the past.

Ask the client if she has had past experiences in counselling or being in therapy. If so, ask her what she found helpful, what was not helpful, and what her experience was like.

Emphasize the client's power to make choices, her freedom to choose, and the extent of your ability to provide further support or refer her to other resources.

Alcohol/Drug Use Continuum
The alcohol/drug use continuum is one guideline that can be used to assess whether a woman is likely to experience problems due to her drinking or other drug use.

NON-USE • EXPERIMENTAL USE • SOCIAL USE • HARMFUL USE • DEPENDENCE

Non-Use is no use of alcohol or other drugs at all.

Experimental Use refers to trying a drug out of curiosity. Based on the experience, the user may or may not continue to use the drug.

Social (or Occasional) Use refers to situations where use is minimal (a drink at dinnertime) or for a short period of time (medication prescribed for a specific health problem).

90.

Harmful Use occurs when a woman experiences negative consequences (e.g., health, legal, social) in her life as a result of her use.

Dependence on a drug occurs with excessive use and when use is continued even though the person is experiencing serious problems because of it.

A woman may be at different points along the continuum at different times in her life.

At any time, a woman could be at one point on the continuum for one drug and at another point for a different drug. Being at one point on the continuum does not necessarily mean that a woman will progress to the next point.

The likelihood of a person developing problems with alcohol and other drugs is often thought of as the "risk" they are at for developing problems. Problems associated with "risk" levels of consumption include health problems, legal problems, social problems, psychological problems, and dependence on the substance.

Dependence can be psychological and/or physical.
- psychological dependence occurs when the user feels a need for the drug — the drug is the central focus of a person's thoughts, emotions and activities
- physical dependence refers to changes that occur in a person's body to adapt to the presence of a drug; if a person no longer takes the drug, she experiences mild (e.g., discomfort) to severe (e.g., convulsions) withdrawal symptoms

Guidelines for Safe Alcohol Use by Women
The likelihood of a person experiencing problems with alcohol increases with:
- the amount of alcohol consumed per week
- the amount of alcohol consumed at one time
- drinking on a daily basis
- having more than one drink per hour
- drinking frequently over a long period
- drinking while taking medication
- drinking and driving (or operating other equipment)

91.

> # LOW-RISK DRINKING FOR WOMEN ...
>
> • no more than one to two drinks on any given day
> • at least one alcohol-free day per week
> • no more than 10 drinks per week
>
> ### but ...
>
> • alcohol may have more of an effect on older women, women in poor health and/or women who are taking medication; so it may be better for them to drink even less
> • no safe drinking levels have been established for pregnant women

[See Appendix at end of this Section for a self-monitoring tool, *"How to Quit Drinking or Cut Down."*]

An Important Note: There is some discrepancy concerning the suggested maximum number of drinks per day. Some researchers suggest a maximum of three drinks per day for women* while others suggest one or two. We have presented the more conservative figures of one or two drinks per day under "Low-Risk Drinking for Women."

*"How to Quit Drinking or Cut Down" in the Appendix — these guidelines are based on research with women who had a serious drinking problem and have cut down to more moderate levels.

When Is the Use of Medications Appropriate?

When taking mood-altering medications to reduce anxiety, ease pain, relieve depression, or induce sleep, the general rule is "less is usually best." There are times, however, when it is beneficial, and even necessary, for people to take medications (over-the-counter and prescription drugs). Medications can help maintain optimum health — but it is important to use them correctly. Examples of the appropriate use of medications include the following conditions:

When a physician has done a thorough assessment of a patient. This assessment might include a physical examination, psychiatric examination, health history, and substance use history of the patient.

- treatment would be based on the diagnosis of the physician that drug therapy is appropriate under the present circumstances (e.g., antidepressants for depression, benzodiazepines for generalized anxiety disorder)
- for a physician to assess whether a woman needs medication, it is important that she abstain from substances for a six-week period; a woman may experience some unpleasant feelings due to the effects of long-term substance use or she may feel the effects of withdrawing from the substances
- the physician and the woman together should set a goal for the length of the prescription: How Long is Treatment Expected to Last? How will the medication be monitored? How can the physician help to ensure that the patient takes the drug as prescribed?
- the physician can decrease the risk of dependency by regularly re-evaluating the need for the drug

Weighing the risks against the benefits and considering a person's quality of life.

- for example, taking painkillers to help cope with short-term, intense pain (e.g., after a root canal procedure) or chronic pain as a result of disease (e.g., cancer)
- for example, taking benzodiazepines (e.g., for acute anxiety or for sleeping) on a short-term basis to cope with a major negative event (e.g., death of a family member) in one's life; but it is important to develop coping strategies at the same time (e.g., through grief counselling)

But if treatment with drugs is chosen:

- it is best to take the lowest amount of medication that works and to take it for the shortest time possible
- it is best to prescribe drugs that have the lowest potential for developing problems or dependence
- it is best to avoid taking more than one type of medication at a time
- special attention should be given to the effects of drugs on pregnant women and older women

93.

- if possible, it is best for the woman and her physician (or counsellor) to deal with the cause of her discomfort rather than just addressing the symptoms

---

Women need to know that it is their right to question. Is it in their best interest to be prescribed medication or are there healthier alternatives?

What about Illegal Drugs?

Guidelines have not been developed around the use of illegal drugs since any use is seen as "risky."

While occasional use of some illegal drugs may not be physically or psychologically harmful, there is a greater risk of a bad reaction to an illegal drug due to impurities or an accidental overdose (since the strength of the drug can vary). In addition, there is always the risk of financial (e.g., spending too much money on drugs) and legal (e.g., being arrested) consequences associated with the use of illegal drugs.

If the client does not want to stop using illegal drugs, you can work with her to ensure that she has access to resources that may reduce the harmful effects associated with her illegal drug use. For example, you could tell her how to obtain clean needles or try to get her into a methadone program.

WHAT Should I Ask about Substance Use?

Essentially, you need to know which drugs a woman uses, how often she uses them, how much she uses, why she uses them (i.e., what triggers her use), and whether she has any concerns about her use or has had any problems as a result of her use.

The following boxes contain **specific questions** you can ask a woman to find out about her use of alcohol, tobacco, caffeine, medications, inhalants, and illegal drugs. They also list potential warning signs that may indicate that a woman is using the substance in a way that could harm her health and well-being — and that further action may be required.

ALCOHOL

Make sure you and the client define "drink" in the same way.

beer   =   wine   =   liquor
340 mL (12 oz.)   140 mL (5 oz.)   40 mL (1.5 oz.)

Questions:

Have you ever had a drink containing alcohol (e.g., beer, wine, liqueur, whisky)?

How often do you have a drink containing alcohol?

How many drinks containing alcohol do you have on a typical day when you are drinking?

Are there days or times of the week when you drink more than usual?

Have you ever driven (or operated other equipment) after having one or more drinks during the previous hour?

Warning Signs:

• drinking every day

• drinking more than one to two drinks on any day or more than 10 drinks a week

• drinking and driving (or operating other machinery)

Remember:

Alcohol may have more of an effect on older women, women in poor health, and women who are taking medications — so it may be better for them to drink even less.

No safe drinking levels have been established for pregnant women.

CAFFEINE

Questions:

Do you drink beverages containing caffeine (e.g., coffee, tea or cola drinks)?

How often do you drink caffeinated drinks?

How many cups (coffee, tea) or glasses (cola drinks) of caffeinated drinks do you drink each day?

Does your caffeine use keep you from sleeping or make you feel jittery or anxious?

Warning Signs:

• regularly drinking the equivalent of more than six to eight cups of coffee a day

• having difficulty sleeping

• being anxious and/or depressed

ILLEGAL DRUGS

Questions:

Have you ever used illegal drugs (e.g., cannabis, cocaine, LSD)?

How often have you taken illegal drugs during the past year?

Do you plan to use illegal drugs again?

Warning Signs:

• having used illegal drugs on more than an experimental basis (one or two times)

• planning to continue to use illegal drugs

INHALANTS

Questions:

Have you ever used an inhalant (e.g., glue, gasoline, paint thinner) to get "high"?

How often have you used inhalants during the past year?

Do you plan to use inhalants again?

Warning Signs:

• having used inhalants on more than an experimental basis (one or two times)

• planning to use inhalants again

TOBACCO

Questions:

Do you smoke? How often?

Are you a social smoker (i.e., do you smoke in groups, at parties)?

How many cigarettes do you usually smoke each day?

Warning Signs:

• smoking every day or smoking regularly

MEDICATIONS

(prescriptions and over-the-counter)

Questions:

Are you currently taking (or have you ever taken) any medications to help you sleep, for anxiety or depression, or for pain? How long have you been taking these medications? How often do you take them?

Do you usually take the prescribed amount of medication or do you sometimes take less than or more than the amount prescribed by the doctor?

Do you take any other prescribed medications?

Do you ever take medication that has been prescribed for someone else (e.g., family member, friend)? Do you ever share your medication with someone else?

Have you ever obtained a prescription for the same drug from more than one doctor, without the other doctor knowing?

Does one doctor know about all the medications you are taking, even if you are prescribed medications by several doctors?

Do you ever have difficulty remembering when to take your medication?

Do you sometimes put your medication in a different bottle from the one given to you by the doctor or pharmacy and then forget to label the bottle?

What over-the-counter medication do you take? Do you take this medication on the advice of a doctor?

Do you ever drink alcohol while you are also taking medication without checking with a doctor?

MEDICATIONS

continued . . .

Warning Signs of Problems with Medication Management:

- not taking medication as prescribed (particularly taking more than prescribed)

- forgetting to take medication or getting confused about which medication is in the container

- not having one doctor who knows about all the medication she takes (e.g., over-the-counter, medication prescribed by another doctor)

Warning Signs of the Inappropriate Use of Medication:

- regularly taking over-the-counter medication without the advice of a doctor

- using medication (e.g., benzodiazepines to help her sleep or for anxiety) regularly for several months or longer

- using medication that has been prescribed for someone else

- drinking alcohol while taking medication without checking with a doctor

You can also ask a woman **general questions** about her substance use and how it affects her life. You may want to ask these questions if a woman is using substances in a way that may be harmful to her health.

- Do you have any questions or concerns about your use of substances?

- Do you find you use alcohol or other drugs to cope with issues in your life (e.g., stress, negative feelings, relationships)?

- Have you experienced any problems or negative consequences (e.g., in your relationships, family, work, health, energy level) because of your substance use?

• Has anyone expressed concern to you about your use of substances?

• Have you ever tried cutting down or quitting? What was it like for you?

• Would you like to make changes in your use of alcohol or other drugs?

Pregnancy is a time when a woman needs to be especially careful about her substance use. Since there is no known safe level of alcohol or other drug use for pregnant women, it would be best that she eliminate her use of substances or take only those medications that are absolutely necessary for her health. If a woman has been taking drugs or drinking regularly while pregnant, reducing or stopping her substance use at any time during the pregnancy will improve her own health as well as the health of the fetus.

It is important to ask a pregnant woman about her use of alcohol and other drugs. But it is just as important to ask her about the substance use of the significant people in her life.

Other people's substance use can affect a pregnant woman and the fetus. For example, a woman may be constantly exposed to second-hand smoke in her home or work environment. Or she may live with someone whose alcohol or other drug use creates additional stress for her and may increase the likelihood that she will also use substances.

Screening Tools
Included in this guidebook [see Appendix at end of this chapter] are the following screening tools that will help you assess if a woman has an alcohol or drug use problem that needs further assessment and possible referral:

> • Health Questionnaire — to assess women's use of substances
> • TWEAK — to identify problems related to alcohol use; the TWEAK is a "woman-friendly" version of the CAGE
> • ICD-10 (International Classification of Diseases, 10th Edition) — to determine if someone is dependent on substances

You can use these screening tools as an interview guide by asking the questions in your own words; or you can ask the questions as written and use the tools as a standardized test.

100.

What Do I Do with this Information?

You and the client may decide that:
1. **She does not have a substance use problem.** For example, the client may not use substances at all, or she may not use them very often, or her substance use may fall within the guidelines for safe or low-risk use.

    What to do? No further action is necessary regarding the client's substance use. However, you may wish to reinforce her current practices by giving her general information about alcohol and other drugs and guidelines for safe use.

or ...

2. **The client uses substances in a way that is cause for concern, but problems have not yet developed.** For example, a woman may drink daily or drink more than one to two drinks on a given day; she may sometimes take more than the prescribed dose of medication; she may take several medications at the same time; she may have used medication for a long period; she may occasionally use illegal drugs; she may drink alcohol while she is taking other drugs; she may be pregnant or breastfeeding.

    What to do? You may need to give the client information about low-risk use of substances and guidelines on how to reduce her substance use. Continue to monitor her substance use with her. Or you and the client may need to explore in more depth under what circumstances she uses substances, which situations trigger her substance use, what are the results of her substance use, and how she feels after she uses substances. Or she may decide that her substance use is not an issue for her. Encouraging the client to keep a daily record of when and how much she uses a particular substance is often helpful in determining how much she is actually using.

or ...

3. **The client's alcohol and/or drug use is harmful.** For example, a woman may say that she is concerned about or has problems with her substance use.

   What to do? It will be necessary to do a more in-depth assessment of the client's substance use as well as of other relevant areas of her life (e.g., how are substances affecting her health and relationships?). It is also important to find out how she feels about stopping or reducing her substance use. If doing an assessment does not fall within your skills or the mandate of your agency, you could discuss this with the client and refer her to an appropriate agency.

   or ...

4. **A woman's family member (e.g., partner) has a substance use problem.** For example, she may tell you that her partner is drinking too much.

   What to do? Encourage a woman to get support for herself through a mutual aid program such as Al Anon or by participating in a program for family members at an alcohol/drug treatment program. In Ontario, assessment/referral services will often see family members and provide them with support and information on available family programs.

Note: It is important not to make assumptions about a woman's life. Every woman is unique. As a counsellor working with women, you will need to take the time to explore each woman's background to better understand her issues and needs.

TAKING ACTION

If you and the client discover that her drinking and/or drug use is harmful, it will be necessary to do a complete assessment of her substance use as well as of other relevant areas of her life. If doing an assessment does not fall within your skills and the mandate of your agency, you could discuss this with the woman and refer her to an appropriate agency. Contact her a few weeks later to see how she is doing. If there is no appropriate agency within your geographic area, you can use the following guidelines to help you through the assessment process.

Doing an In-Depth Assessment

It is important to ask a woman about all aspects of her life and not just about her substance use. This enables both of you to look at issues that may have contributed to her substance use and may need to be addressed in treatment. It will also make you aware of issues (e.g., financial, legal, child care) that could limit the treatment options available to a particular woman.

The *"What to Include"* section below is intended as a guideline for areas that could be included in an in-depth assessment. Counsellors and agencies that do not already ask about most or all of these content areas are encouraged to integrate the *"What to Include"* components into their existing assessment procedures. Most content areas are generic; however, some are more likely to be relevant to women's lives (e.g., prescription drug use, eating issues, physical or sexual violence).

At first, a woman may simply give you a general overview of her life. But as she starts to trust you more, you will find that the information she gives you will become more specific.

If you feel a woman's use of substances is at such a level that it may be creating problems in her life, you might want to ask her more detailed questions. The next section, *"When to Be Concerned about a Woman's Substance Use,"* includes lists of symptoms that, if present, may indicate a woman has a potential or an already-serious problem

WHY DO AN ASSESSMENT?

The purpose for doing an assessment is to:

1. obtain broad background information about a woman's life situation

2. develop a personal action plan together with the client — based on information obtained in 1

3. make the best referral possible

4. decide on a follow-up plan

WHAT TO INCLUDE

- general concerns:
  - why the client has come to you
- alcohol and other drug use history: (including caffeine, tobacco, medications):
  - the amount of alcohol or drugs used
  - how often the substances are used
  - the pattern of substance use (e.g., occasionally, on weekends, regularly, daily, binging)
  - if needles are shared or reused
  - how dependent the client is on particular substances, is there more than one substance
  - what triggers substance use
  - the consequences of substance use
  - previous history of treatment
- physical health history:
  - physical examination
  - general health (including memory difficulties, blackouts)
  - sexual health (gynecology, pregnancies, sexually transmitted infections)
  - HIV, Hepatitis B and C
  - eating patterns
  - exercise
- mental health history:
  - current problems
  - which came first: mental health issue or substance use
  - suicidal thoughts or attempts
  - previous history of treatment
- family history:
  - parents', partner's alcohol and other drug use
  - family disruption (parental divorce, death in family)
  - parental neglect
  - emotional, physical and/or sexual violence against a parent and/or herself
- sexual orientation
- living arrangements

- social support:
  - the nature and extent of social support (family, partner, friends, self-help group, counsellor)
  - child care arrangements, care of other dependents (while she receives treatment)
- history of violence (i.e., experiencing emotional, physical, sexual violence):
  - as a child and/or adult
  - who the abuser was/is
- ethnocultural background:
  - ethnocultural group
  - country of origin
  - status when coming to Canada (landed immigrant, refugee)
  - language most comfortable speaking
- financial issues:
  - does she have enough money (e.g., for child care, transportation)?
  - main source of income
- legal issues:
  - custody of children
  - record of arrests (e.g., for driving while intoxicated, processing illegal drugs, engaging in prostitution)
  - charges pending
- education or job issues:
  - level of education
  - literacy level
  - current and past job descriptions
  - problems at school or work
  - need for upgrading or retraining
  - unemployment
- life events and issues (these issues may come out in other content areas):
  - losses (e.g., children leaving home, death of partner, breakup of relationship, miscarriage)
  - personal habits
  - leisure activities
- future goals (e.g., reducing or stopping her substance use, dealing with all substances she uses or with only one, making changes in other areas of her life)

with substance use. You could use the information in the table as a checklist (i.e., has the woman mentioned experiencing any of these problems?); or you could use them as a guide by mentioning these symptoms and asking her if she has ever, or is currently, experiencing some of these problems.

Note: Some women may have difficulty sharing and speaking about painful aspects of their lives. In such cases, it is important to respect a woman's comfort level. It is better to have less information about a woman than to have her not come back because she feels she had to tell you things she really did not want to reveal, she feels she has no more defences, she does not want to be seen as a bundle of problems, or she feels embarrassed or ashamed about what she has already told you.

Looking at the many factors in a woman's life helps place her substance use within a broader context. It also makes her more aware of how her substance use is closely connected to everything else that is going on — or has gone on — in her life.

When to Be Concerned about a Woman's Substance Use

A woman may not necessarily tell you all the details of her life or she may not feel that she has specific problems related to her substance use. In the field of substance use, the term, "denial", is often used to describe a client who the counsellor believes is resistant to admitting that she has problems with alcohol or other drug use. But there may be other reasons why a woman is resistant to saying she has problems around substance use and discussing them openly with you. For example, the two of you may not have established a relationship yet; the client may still be setting appropriate boundaries; she may be afraid that you will contact external reporting agencies if you know the true extent of her substance use (e.g., Children's Aid Societies); or she may not agree with your suggestions at this point in your relationship.

Various signs may indicate that a woman is experiencing problems in her life — physical health, mental health, family, school or work, financial or legal — as a result of her alcohol or other drug

105.

Problem Area	Potential Signs of Problem Use	Serious Problems
Physical Health	• hangover (e.g., not feeling well, red eyes, hand tremor) • alcohol or mouthwash on breath • sudden weight loss • irregular menstrual cycle • chronic complaints (e.g., sleep disturbances, stomach problems, heart burn, high blood pressure) • frequent falls, accidents, cuts or burns • significant change in hygiene and appearance	• blackouts (no memory of events) • ulcer • liver disease • stroke • brain damage • heart disease • overdose
Mental Health	• forgetting things • difficulty concentrating • being worried about using substances • using substances to cope with stress • emotional distress (e.g., confusion, depression, anxiety, mood swings, self-mutilation, suicidal thoughts or attempts)	• permanent memory damage • feeling hopeless, worthless, depressed • significant changes in attitude, personality • obsession with substances • suicidal thoughts or attempts
Relationships/ Social	• disputes with family, friends • isolation from family, friends • notable changes in relationships with significant others and friends (e.g., seeking new friends with similar substance use patterns) • loss of interest in activities not directly related to substance use • children reluctant to bring friends home • children develop school or behavioral problems • family history of abstinence or problematic substance use	• family breakup • family violence (e.g., by a partner, neglect of or violence against a child) • health problems in children due to parental substance use (e.g., alcohol-related birth effects)
School or Work	• significant change in school or work performance • late for school or work • disappearing in afternoon • missing classes or work • hung over at school or work	• accident at work • suspension from school, quitting school • job loss
Financial or Legal	• spending too much money on alcohol and/or other drugs • drinking and driving (or operating other equipment, such as an iron) • frequent minor auto accidents	• gambling • getting into debt • stealing • being charged with impaired driving or having a serious auto collision

106.

use. Some of the more common signs are listed in the opposite table. Remember that these are possible indicators of problematic alcohol or other drug use but could also be signs of something else.

Stages of Change

Some clients may not need to change. They may not use alcohol or other drugs at all. Or they may use them in a way that is not likely to create problems for themselves or other people.

For those women who could benefit from changing their substance use, however, it is important to know how they perceive their substance use and how ready they are to change their substance use.

Women might be at different stages of change for different substances they are using. Or they may not see the use of one of the drugs as a problem (e.g., medications prescribed by a physician).

Understanding the stages of change will enable you to help the client begin the process of change. It will help her:
• be aware of both the positive and negative impact that substance use has on her life
• see that she can make positive changes in her life
• understand that both external and internal factors affect how these changes take place
• take personal responsibility for making changes

PRECONTEMPLATION
◆
CONTEMPLATION
◆
PREPARATION
◆
ACTION
◆
MAINTENANCE
◆
TERMINATION

When a client first comes to see a counsellor, she could be in any one of the stages of change — depending on why she is seeking help.

A client's readiness to change is an important factor in how willing she is to address her substance use problem. Knowing where a client is in the stages of change assists the counsellor in deciding which intervention strategies are appropriate and if, and where, the client should be referred for treatment.

When she is deciding to change her behavior, a woman may move through the stages of change in either direction and may move back and forth more than once. As a counsellor, it is important that you support her throughout this process.

Understanding and working with a woman using the "stages of change" model is a client-centred approach. The client moves at her own pace and chooses her own goals rather than meeting the counsellor's goals and expectations.

A description of each stage of change — along with suggested responses from the counsellor — is outlined below.

Adapted from Prochaska et al. (1994).

PRECONTEMPLATION

"I don't want to change and don't need to change."

Client
- not considering change *("I like smoking.")*
- is usually in counselling due to pressure or force by significant others, employers, or the legal system
- does not recognize a need for change; may deny there are problems *("I'm not addicted. I can quit any time I want to.")*
- surprised by concern of family members, friends *("I don't understand why you think I have a drinking problem." "It's their problem.")*
- may not want to look at her substance use
- may participate in a limited manner or withdraw from counselling

Counsellor Response
- try to find out:
  - what has brought the client for counselling
  - her feelings around being forced to come
  - how she sees her substance use and its effects
  - if the client has any concerns for which she would like support or referral
- give objective feedback by going over the results of an assessment, and physical examination
- show the client that you respect her and are interested in her point of view
- talk about how the client's substance use can affect her life both positively and negatively
- give the client some choices (e.g., being able to choose her next appointment time with you)

CONTEMPLATION

"I'd like to change. Maybe I will one day."

Client

- considering change — but not ready to commit to change and may not believe she can change *("I've thought about smoking less but it helps me relax.")*
- recognizes some of the negative effects of her alcohol or other drug use but also feels her use of substances plays a positive role in her life
- feels it would create more stress in her life if she quit right now

Counsellor Response

- assist the client in moving beyond her feelings of uncertainty to a state of cognitive dissonance (internal conflict resulting from knowing that her substance use stands in the way of reaching her life goals); help her recognize how her substance use does not fit in with her values and beliefs
- explore the positive and negative aspects of substance use in the client's life
- help the client understand her mixed feelings about her substance use
- work with the client to show her that change is possible — help her to overcome barriers that she foresees, explore with her what could be changed and how

PREPARATION

"I want to change but I haven't decided how to go about it."

Client

- getting ready to change
- feels more confident about her ability to change
- shifting focus away from problems of the past and onto how she wants her life to be in the future *("If I stop going to bars with my friends, I'll have more time to do other things that I really enjoy and that add to my overall well-being.")*
- searching for the most appropriate way to turn her wishes into action
- talks to family and friends about the desired change and asks for their support

Counsellor Response

- continue the process of working with the client to look at herself, her life and her substance use in new ways
- encourage the client to focus on the positive aspects of change; for example, she could make a list of how changing her behavior will benefit various aspects of her life
- help the client develop strategies to make changing her substance use a priority in her life

109.

ACTION

"I'm changing my behavior and replacing it with activities that are better for me."

Client

- starting to change (*"I've cut down on the number of cigarettes I smoke a day."*)
- expresses some urgency in wanting to begin the change process and see results right away (*"I need to get into a treatment program right away."*)
- changing her usual pattern of behavior and now has to function without relying on her normal way of coping
- is replacing her substance use with healthier alternatives
- self-esteem increases

Counsellor Response

- encourage the client's desire to change
- help the client develop confidence in her ability to change
- assist the client in accepting the responsibility for making changes
- do a complete assessment of the client so you both understand what the client's problems are, her strengths and weaknesses — from this you can work together to develop goals for her that are realistic and achievable
- explore with the client what has helped her make changes in the past (i.e., coping strategies)
- help the client decide what healthy, alternative activities she would like to pursue and how she can fit them into her schedule

MAINTENANCE

"I'm keeping up my changed behavior and lifestyle."

Client

- reinforcing the change (*"I try to stay away from places where I used to use drugs."*)
- integrating new skills and behaviors learned during the Action stage, including:
  - relating to others (sharing, communicating well, meeting each other's needs)
  - learning how to ask for support (to avoid isolation)
  - making decisions (making choices, seeing the links between values, goals, means and end results)
  - exploring new ways of learning
  - doing other things (*"I went for a walk instead of reaching for a cigarette."*)
  - reinforcing the selection of alternative coping techniques

Counsellor Response

- help the client develop a balanced lifestyle
- help the client explore alternatives, options, and goals (e.g., more schooling, volunteer work, mother's support group)
- help the client identify potential relapse situations and plan coping strategies to avoid relapse
- encourage the client to continue and maintain the process of change
- identify and reinforce positive changes in the client's behavior (e.g., through ongoing support, such as a continuing care group and/or individual counselling)
- refer the client to self-help/mutual-aid groups

TERMINATION

"I've changed for good!"

Client
- has a more positive attitude and self-image
- is never tempted to resume her substance use regardless of the situation or emotions she is feeling that may have triggered her use in the past (*"I no longer feel any desire to take drugs."*)
- feels confident she can cope with any situation without lapsing
- has an overall healthier lifestyle

Counsellor Response
- congratulate the client on her good work in changing her substance use

Changing behaviors is not as simple as moving directly through a series of stages (e.g., from precontemplation to termination) from one point to another. Rather, it is common for a person to relapse or experience lapses or slips in behavior at least once along the way. This is a normal part of the recovery process that involves making

RELAPSE (OR LAPSE)

"Oops, I slipped up for a while."

Client
- not maintaining change (*"I couldn't cope with flashbacks about my childhood and took tranquillizers to calm myself down."*)

Counsellor Response
- be empathetic
- help the client view the lapse as an opportunity for learning rather than as a failure
- assist the client in becoming aware of what triggers her use of drugs, of what her other options are
- help the client cope with feelings of guilt (which can lead to further use)
- help the client focus on her strengths and what has worked for her in the past to reduce or eliminate her substance use
- assess the client's current needs — does she require more substance-focused counselling and/or counselling to address other life problems (e.g., trauma issues)?

significant life changes and learning new skills. A one-time episode of using alcohol or other drugs at problem levels after a period of abstinence or reduced use is usually called a "lapse" while longer or repeated episodes of problematic substance use are usually labelled a "relapse."

Next Steps after Assessment

You have done an in-depth assessment with the client. What next? That depends on what you and the woman have learned about her substance use and its effects on her life, and her readiness to change her substance use and her current life situation.

Depending on how serious her substance use problem is and depending on your knowledge and skill levels and the mandate of your agency, you and the client may decide that she is in a good position to help herself, that it would be more beneficial if you continue working with her, that she needs immediate assistance (e.g., at a detoxification centre), or that she should consider going to a specialized substance use program. Outlined below are a number of possible situations.

The client is able to help herself.

If a woman is in the early stages of developing a drinking problem, for example, you may both feel that she can reduce her alcohol use or stop drinking altogether on her own without the help of you or anyone else. Self-help materials are available that she can work with to achieve her goals. It might be best if you review the materials with her to help her choose a program best suited to her particular needs, life situation, and goals. For example, *Saying When* by Sanchez-Craig is suitable for someone who is not alcohol dependent, is not going through a personal crisis, and does not have problems with drugs other than alcohol.

It is best if you continue working with the client.

The client may decide that she would like to continue working with you. For instance, she may still be exploring her substance use issues and options for change; or you may both feel that your skills and the mandate of your agency best suit her needs at this time. It is important to work with a woman at her own pace (e.g., she may be willing to work on one substance now but not on others) and to help her set priorities (e.g., she may first need to find child care or suitable housing).

The client may need help right away because of her current situation.

(a) The client may need a referral to a detoxification centre or to a hospital emergency department if she is using substances heavily and does not feel she can stop without more support, if she had serious withdrawal symptoms when she stopped using substances in the past, if she is using several substances at the same time and there would be harmful consequences if she stopped using them without medical supervision (e.g., alcohol and barbiturates), or if the people she lives with are heavy substance users. If you are not sure which option is best for a woman, it would be best to first contact the detoxification centre or consult with a physician.

(b) The client may need a referral to a shelter or help in developing a plan of action if she is living with an abusive partner or family or in any other situation where she is in danger.

(c) The client may need a referral to temporary housing if she is living on the street or in any other situation that does not lend support to her decision to cut down on or stop using substances.

The client may need to go to a specialized substance use program.

A variety of treatment programs and services are available across Canada although there are more options to choose from in larger centres than in smaller communities. Some services may be suitable for a broad range of people while others may be designed for a particular group (e.g., women, men, younger people, older people, specific ethnocultural group, people involved with the legal system). Services range from self-help and mutual aid groups to live-in treatment settings (although this option is seldom necessary). In making a decision about referral, it is important to match the client's needs to the treatment services that are available. To find out about options in Ontario, for example, you can call the Drug and Alcohol Registry of Treatment (DART) at 1-800-565-8603.

Generally speaking, some treatment options are more suitable than others for women. Whether a program is available and accessible are other factors that will have to be considered. The following table lists the many treatment options available.

Note: When helping a woman consider available treatment options that are appropriate for her situation, support a woman in choosing the option that is least disruptive to her life. If a woman can achieve her goals through an outpatient (live-at-home) treatment intervention, then that is preferable to attending a live-in program. If a woman can achieve her goals by herself or through a self-help program, then that is preferable to attending daily or weekly individual or group counselling sessions.

LIVE-AT-HOME CHOICES

Choices	Designed For	Common Features	Usual Length	Requirements
Assessment and Referral	Someone who may have a problem with substance use; or another person who is concerned about someone else's substance use	• exploration of how alcohol and other drugs affect the client's life • development (with the client) of a plan for treatment • helping the client access the most suitable treatment service • linking the client with other community services • providing support to the client before and after treatment • advocacy with other community agencies to obtain services to support the client and information for the client's family	One or two two-hour assessment interviews	• attendance at one or two appointments • participation in an interview of up to two hours • not be under the influence of alcohol or other drugs for the appointment (unless it is medication prescribed by a doctor)
Weekly Counselling	Someone who shows early signs of having a problem with alcohol or other drug use or who shows signs of relapsing	• exploration of how alcohol and other drugs affect the client's life • development (with the client) of goals around the use of alcohol and other drugs • education about the risks of alcohol and other drug use • skills training for leading a healthy, balanced life • linkages to other community services • help to avoid a relapse • one-on-one support and guidance; group counselling sessions • programs for seniors may provide counselling in the client's home • counselling in a range of life areas • readings and assignments • support and information for the client's family or referral to family support services	One or two sessions per week for one to six months	• attendance at regularly scheduled sessions • not be under the influence of alcohol or other drugs for the sessions (unless it is medication prescribed by a doctor)

LIVE-AT-HOME CHOICES *continued ...*

Choices	Designed For	Common Features	Usual Length	Requirements
Daytime or Evening Counselling	Someone who has problems with or is dependent on substances	• education about the risks of alcohol and other drug use • skills training for leading a healthy, balanced life • one-on-one support and guidance; group-counselling sessions • support and information for the client's family or referral to family support services • planning (with the client) for what will happen after the treatment program is finished • help to avoid a relapse • linkages to mutual aid groups (e.g., Alcoholics Anonymous)	Two to five hours each weekday for two to five weeks	• attendance at daily activities • not have used alcohol or any other drugs for several days before entering the treatment program • not be using alcohol or other drugs during the treatment program
Continuing Care	Clients who have participated in outpatient, day or residential treatment programs	• refresher course in skills training for leading a healthy, balanced life • one-on-one support and guidance; group-counselling sessions • help to avoid a relapse • linkages to mutual aid groups • use of self-help books	Several months to several years, as required	• previously completed a substance use treatment program
Mutual Aid Group	Someone who was dependent on alcohol or other drugs and requires group support to not use substances	• socializing with other people who are recovering from alcohol or other drug problems • members support each other by sharing experiences, strengths and hope • structured program of recovery (e.g., 12-step program of Alcoholics Anonymous) • social activities where there are no alcohol or other drugs available • there are no dues or fees; voluntary contributions from the members support the group • there may be role models who "sponsor" or serve as mentors	Meetings last one to two hours and are held on a regular basis in most communities across Canada	• desire to stop drinking or taking other drugs • respect for the principles of the group

LIVE-AT-HOME CHOICES *continued ...*

Choices	Designed For	Common Features	Usual Length	Requirements
Individual Self-Help	Someone who wants to quit or cut down on her drinking and is not dependent on alcohol, is not going through a personal crisis, and does not have problems with drugs other than alcohol	• use of self-help materials to give the client suggested methods (that other people have found helpful) to reduce or stop her alcohol use • privacy and anonymity • flexibility (e.g., client does not need transportation or child care and she can work it into her life without disrupting her daily schedule)	Until the client reaches her long-term goals	• following the program outlined in the materials • desire to quit or cut down on her alcohol use

117.

LIVE-IN CHOICES

Choices	Designed For	Common Features	Usual Length	Requirements
Detoxification	Someone who wants to withdraw from alcohol or other drugs with supervision and support	• provision of shelter, meals and support • monitoring of client's withdrawal symptoms • access to nearby emergency medical services • information about different treatment programs and help in accessing them • linkages to mutual aid groups • in rural areas, detoxification services may be available in several different settings (e.g., at home)	Three to five days	• not drinking or taking other drugs (unless prescribed by a doctor) on the premises • not being violent • not being in need of immediate medical attention
Short-Term Residential	Someone who has problems with or is dependent on substances, has a long history of problems with alcohol and/or other drugs, and/or has not been successful in a non-residential treatment program	• education about the risks of alcohol and other drug use • skills training for leading a healthy, balanced life • one-on-one support and guidance; group-counselling sessions • support and information for the client's family or referral to family support services • planning (with the client) for what will happen after the treatment program is finished • sports and recreation • help to avoid a relapse • linkages to mutual-aid groups	Up to one month	• not have used alcohol or any other drugs for several days before entering the treatment program • not drinking or taking other drugs while in the program • participation in education and treatment activities

LIVE-IN CHOICES *continued...*

Choices	Designed For	Common Features	Usual Length	Requirements
Long-Term Residential	Someone who has problems with or is dependent on substances, has a long history of problems with alcohol and/or other drugs, has not been successful in a non-residential treatment program, and has a poor job history, poor social skills, and inadequate housing	• provision of help in re-entering the community (e.g., social support, job retraining, housing) • education about the risks of alcohol and other drug use • skills training for leading a healthy, balanced life • one-on-one support and guidance; group-counselling sessions • support and information for the client's family or referral to family support services • planning (with the client) for what will happen after the treatment program is finished • sports and recreation • help to avoid a relapse • linkages to mutual-aid groups	Six weeks to six months	• completion of detoxification (i.e., having no alcohol or other drugs in the body) • not drinking or taking other drugs while in the treatment program • participation in education and treatment activities
Therapeutic Community	Someone who is trying to rebuild her life without the use of alcohol or other drugs	• strict rules and rigid schedules • job skills training • creation of a family unit for clients • the majority of clients have been dependent on cocaine or heroin • provision of help in re-entering the community • education about the risks of alcohol and other drug use • skills training for leading a healthy, balanced life • one-on-one support and guidance; group-counselling sessions • planning (with the client) for what will happen after the treatment program is finished • sports and recreation • help to avoid a relapse • linkages to mutual-aid groups	Six to fifteen months	• completion of detoxification (i.e., having no alcohol or other drugs in the body) • having had a medical and psychiatric examination • participation in a rigid schedule of activities • helping to take care of the treatment setting (e.g., doing chores)

119.

LIVE-IN CHOICES *continued...*

Choices	Designed For	Common Features	Usual Length	Requirements
Supportive (Halfway) Housing	Someone who has completed a live-in treatment program and needs a bridge, or intermediate step, before living on her own again	• home-like atmosphere • provision of help in re-entering the community • practise in skills for leading a healthy, balanced life • access to one-on-one support and guidance and to group-counselling sessions • help to avoid a relapse • linkages to mutual aid groups	Six months to one year	• completion of detoxification (i.e., having no alcohol or other drugs in the body) • involvement in activities outside the house (e.g., school, work) • financial contribution (if possible) to food and housing

Adapted from Addiction Research Foundation (1994)

SELECTING A TREATMENT PROGRAM

Outlined below are a number of different areas (along with specific questions) that you and the client should consider in selecting the treatment program best suited to her particular needs. *[Adapted from information provided by Bev Cain, Drug and Alcohol Registry of Treatment (Ontario) and Bonnie Orvidas, Thames Valley Addiction Assessment and Referral Centre London, Ontario.]*

Note: *Refer to* "Access Issues," "Program Issues," *and* "Counselling Issues" *in Chapter 3 for a discussion of many of the issues identified on the following pages.*

Basic InformationYou Need to Know about the Client
• age
• gender
• sexual orientation
• language preference
• ethnocultural background
• substance(s) used — low-risk use, problem use, dependence
• mobility, vision or hearing problems — are specialized services required?
• developmental handicaps — are specialized services required?
• living arrangements
• psychiatric diagnosis — is there a need for a program offering treatment for both substance use and a mental health problem? is medication being used?
• other co-occurring problems (e.g., eating issues, violence, HIV, AIDS, self-harming behaviors)
• legal problems — is the client on probation or parole? does the client have court dates to attend?
• service preference — does the client prefer a mixed group or one that serves a particular population (e.g., French, Aboriginal, women, youth, dual diagnosis)?
• barriers to getting help — e.g., are there concerns over physical safety, fears that children might be taken away?

121.

How to Find Out what Is Available in Your Community

Once a client has been assessed and it has been decided that she will be referred for treatment, you can check various resources to find out what is available to best meet her needs. Resources include:

- Canadian Centre for Substance Abuse
    - Directory of Alcohol and Drug Treatment Resources
    - Directory of Substance Abuse Organizations in Canada
    - Inventory of Addictions Treatment Services for Women in Canada
- Drug and Alcohol Registry of Treatment (DART) (Ontario) 1-800-565-8603. Provides up-to-date information about alcohol and other drug treatment services across Ontario (available in different languages)
- assessment and referral centres (in the local area)

For information about services in each province, see the list of provincial organizations in *If You Want More Information* at the end of this publication.

Making yourself familiar with the services to which you refer a woman helps her choose a program best suited to her needs and hopefully increases her comfort level about participating in the program.

Note: It may take some time for a woman to get into the service that both of you have identified as being most suitable. Stay in touch with her during this period, continue to offer your support, and link her up with an available mutual-aid group, if appropriate.

Questions to Ask about Access

- How do women gain access to the program (i.e., what are the admission procedures)? Is there a specialized assessment process for women?
- Does the woman have to travel to the program for intake? Does she have to call in weekly for pre-treatment? Can she call collect?
- Are there physical barriers to access (e.g., stairs)?
- How long does the woman need to be substance-free before starting the program? Is there random screening for substances?
- Is there a woman's detoxification centre close to the treatment centre?
- Are pregnant women accepted? Under what conditions?

- Is there a family component to the treatment program that allows family members to actively participate in the client's care? If her partner attends, is child care available?
- Does the program provide or make arrangements for child care? What are they?
- Does the program have reliable admission dates or do they change? Does the program provide a confirmed admission date well in advance so women can prepare adequately? *[Note: This is especially an issue for women with children or women who may need to plan time away from work or school.]*
- Are any costs associated with the program?
- Can women of all ages attend?
- What are counsellors' experience, knowledge, and attitudes around working with lesbians or bisexual women?
- Are appropriate language and cultural support services provided?
- Is a continuing care program available?

Questions to Ask about the Program

- What kind of staff does the agency employ (recovered, professional, combination, outside medical or psychiatric consultants, racial/cultural diversity)? How involved are they in the actual program?
- What is the basis or philosophy of the treatment program? Is attendance at Alcoholics Anonymous or another self-help group a mandatory requirement? How many meetings a week?
- Is a medical examination required? Can this be done by the woman's physician or is it done at the treatment centre?
- What does the program offer for women clients? Is there:
  - individual assessment and counselling
  - communications skills training
  - assertiveness training
  - stress and crisis management education
  - skills training to develop self-esteem
  - support system development
  - parenting skills
  - financial management education
- Is psychiatric counselling available? Are psychiatric medications acceptable? Which ones?

123.

- Is counselling available, and in what format, for women who have experienced physical and/or sexual violence?
- Is there treatment for eating issues? In what format? What happens if a woman's eating issue or self-harming behavior gets worse when she is substance-free? Will she be asked to leave the program?
- If there is not a woman-only program, are women counsellors available for individual counselling? What is the men-to-women ratio in the program?
- In mixed-group (men and women) programs, are some group sessions for women only? How often?
- Is there anything in the program that helps a woman put her alcohol or other drug use in a societal context (i.e., taking into account how women are viewed and treated in society)?
- What if a woman starts using substances again while she is in the program? Will she be asked to leave?
- Is there understanding and support for lesbians and bisexual women? Are specific groups available? Will a woman have support if she decides to "come out"?
- Are there appropriate policies and procedures to assist HIV-positive clients?
- Is medical care available? Are experts in women's health issues available? Is the doctor at the treatment centre a man or a woman? *[Note: Some women do not want a medical done by an unknown physician and/or by a male physician.]*
- Are there any medical or psychological risks associated with the program (e.g., the requirement to stop all drug use immediately including the use of necessary medications)?
- Are programs and services culturally appropriate (i.e., ideas, philosophy of approach)?
- How is diversity (e.g., age, sexual orientation) among the women responded to and accommodated?
- Is there a compulsory religious component to the program?
- Is there a spiritual component to the program?
- Is there an active physical education or sports component to the program? What level of physical activity is expected? What takes place in fitness classes? Is it mandatory?
- What happens in the evenings and on weekends? Are there any planned activities? How rigid and controlling is the program

when not in session? Are women free to go out of the centre? Are they trusted to be responsible? *[**Note:** Control issues can be offensive to women and remind them of unpleasant life experiences.]*

- What about visiting hours? Can a woman's children come and see her? Can she go home on weekends? Can she leave the centre with her family and friends when they visit?
- What about phone calls? Can a woman receive and/or make phone calls to family members? When? Is it a pay phone? Is it private?
- Does the client have to cook meals, clean or do other chores?
- How much privacy is there in the program? Do women share bed-rooms and/or bathrooms?
- Does the client have to sign a contract or any other document? Is the client asked for pledges of money, property or other assets?
- Is there an advocacy component to the program whereby a client receives help in making connections to other services?
- Is there a continuing care program? Who takes part in it? For how long?

APPENDIX

How To Quit Drinking or Cut Down
[Source: Sanchez-Craig (1995)]

What is Moderate Drinking?
Moderate drinking is drinking at a level that does not interfere with your health, your relationships, or responsibilities. It is also drinking at a level that does not hurt yourself or others. Women whose drinking was causing them problems and who now drink sensibly follow these guidelines*. They:
- Don't drink daily — successful clients typically abstained about three days a week.
- Don't drink more than three standard drinks per day.
- Don't drink more than nine standard drinks a week — most of the time, successful clients stayed well below these limits.
- Don't drink more than one drink per hour — this helps avoid intoxication.
- Never drink to cope with problems.
- Don't make alcohol an important part of recreation activities.

Never drink during or before risky activities (e.g., when driving, boating, swimming or doing any task that *might* endanger lives).

Important Note: *These guidelines are based on the drinking styles of women clients rated "successful" one to two years after the program when they reported that their drinking was not causing them any problems. The guidelines may change as more research on moderate drinking becomes available. Remember that all drinking has risks, and the lower your drinking, the lower your risks.*

WHAT IS A DRINK?

one standard drink is equal to: 45 mL (1.5 oz) spirits, 85 mL (3.0 oz) fortified wine, 140 mL (5.0 oz) table wine, 341 mL (12.0 oz bottle) regular beer

---

Steps to Quitting or Cutting Down

1. *Decide on your long term goal and how to achieve it.*
- Cut down gradually until you successfully reach moderate drinking or abstinence.
- Start drinking moderately or quit drinking altogether and continue to abstain or drink moderately.
- Abstain from alcohol for two weeks and then decide whether you want to continue to abstain or become a moderate drinker.

2. *If you choose moderate drinking, specify your goal.*
If you choose moderate drinking, it is best to stay within the guidelines specified above. Specify your goal as follows:

Maximum number of days you will drink in any week
_____ days

Maximum number of drinks you will take on any day
_____ drinks

Maximum number of drinks you will have each week
_____ drinks

Risky Situations
Record situations in which you may be tempted to go over your set limits.

_____
_____
_____
_____
_____
_____
_____

3. *Keep track of your drinking*
Keep a daily record of your drinking and non-drinking days.
Clients who record their drinking every day for at least three months are most successful in reaching and maintaining their goal.

127.

Drinking Diary

My Goal for Week #_____
Maximum Number of Drinks per Day _____
Maximum Number of Drinking Days This Week _____
Maximum Number of Drinks This Week _____

	M	T	W	T	F	S	S	Total
12 oz bottles beer								
5 oz glasses wine								
3 oz glasses fortified wine								
1.5 oz shots liquor								
Total Drinks per Day								

4. *Pace your drinking*

- Measure your drinks.
- Dilute your drinks to lower the concentration of alcohol (e.g., adding soda to a glass of wine to make a "spritzer").
- Sip your drinks; don't gulp.
- Allow at least one hour between drinks.
- Alternate alcoholic drinks with soft drinks, juice or water.
- Avoid drinking without having some food.
- Avoid cocktails that contain more than one alcoholic beverage.

Successful moderate drinkers often switch to beverages with less alcohol, such as light wine or light beer.

128.

5. *Plan ahead to avoid heavy drinking*

When you are beginning to abstain or drinking moderately, you need to plan in advance how you are going to deal with pressure to drink in social situations.

Before going to a social event, you should always:
• decide whether you will drink at all
• plan effective ways of saying "no" to yourself and "no" to others

Other strategies can include:
• asking someone you trust to help you stay on target (e.g., by reminding you of your limit or serving you diluted drinks)
• finding a simple way to count the drinks you consume (e.g., by moving a coin from one pocket to another)
• be ready to use a good excuse for not drinking (e.g., "I'm not drinking tonight" "No thanks, I am driving").

6. *Develop leisure and other free-time activities*

People who successfully learn to abstain or moderate their drinking make a deliberate effort to replace the hours they spent drinking with other activities. Do things that give you pleasure:
• go for a walk
• see a movie
• read a book
• listen to music
• learn a new skill
• join a club

7. *Cope with problems without drinking*

Problems of daily life can upset your plan to abstain or drink moderately. These problems can range from minor irritations to personal catastrophes. Problems that threaten progress often involve:
• ongoing conflicts with another person
• experiencing negative feelings

Because you cannot predict the specific problems, it is wise to have a problem-solving strategy to tackle a problem as it comes along.

129.

Here are some steps to approach problems of daily life in a systematic way:

- Identify the problem — how do you feel about it, how do you usually handle it and what are the consequences of your actions?

- Consider new approaches — think of new ways to handle the situation.

- Select the most promising approach — ask yourself if this approach is going to have positive results and why. Is it practical and realistic?

- Assess whether your new approach worked — did it get the results you wanted? Could you have done something else to make your approach more effective?

If your approach did not work, or you were unable to put it into practice, don't give up. Try another one. There is always more than one solution to a problem.

8. *Maintain your progress*
Strategies you have already learned include:
- keep your drink diary
- pace your drinking
- plan ahead to avoid drinking more than your limit
- develop leisure activities that do not involve drinking
- cope with problems without drinking

New Strategies
Occasional slips — when you do not meet your goal, when you drink too much — are not uncommon. Don't give up or get discouraged. Learn from your experience. Take a fresh look at your coping strategies and goals.

Give yourself regular check-ups. Review your progress every three months and review your drinking and the strategies you are using to reduce or quit drinking.

130.

Screening Tools

It is important to tell the client that screening for substance use is a routine procedure for all clients — whether you think they may have a substance use problem or not.

Women's Health and Drug Use Questionnaire

The client can complete the Women's Health and Drug Use Questionnaire on her own. Answers are not scored. Rather, the questionnaire is one more tool that you can use to open up a discussion with a woman about her use of alcohol and other drugs.

WOMEN'S HEALTH AND DRUG USE QUESTIONNAIRE

1. Have you ever had any of the following health problems?

	Yes	No
(a) anemia or other blood disorders	☐	☐
(b) high blood pressure	☐	☐
(c) yellow jaundice or liver disease	☐	☐
(d) vomiting blood or other stomach problems	☐	☐
(e) inflammation of the pancreas or pancreatitis	☐	☐
(f) infertility (i.e., problems getting pregnant)	☐	☐
(g) problems with your ovaries	☐	☐
(h) problems with your fallopian tubes	☐	☐

2. Which, if any, of the following describes your usual menstrual periods? (If menopause has taken place, answer for your menstrual periods before menopause.) *Check all that apply.*

(a) irregular	☐
(b) painful	☐
(c) accompanied by nausea	☐
(d) accompanied by depression	☐
(e) premenstrual tension	☐

---

3. Have you had periods of feeling hopeless, blue
   or depressed? At those times, did you: Yes   No

   (a) lose your appetite?   ❑   ❑
   (b) lose or gain weight?   ❑   ❑
   (c) lose interest in things that usually interest you?   ❑   ❑
   (d) stay in bed all day or go all day without
       getting dressed?   ❑   ❑
   (e) have spells when you could not seem to
       stop crying?   ❑   ❑
   (f) have difficulty sleeping?   ❑   ❑
   (g) feel this way for one week or longer?   ❑   ❑

4. When you are depressed or nervous,
   do you find any of the following   Helpful   Not   Never
   helpful to feel better or to relax?   Helpful Tried

   (a) smoking cigarettes   ❑   ❑   ❑
   (b) working harder than usual at home
       or job   ❑   ❑   ❑
   (c) taking a tranquillizer
       (i.e., benzodiazepine)   ❑   ❑   ❑
   (d) taking some other kind of pill
       or medication   ❑   ❑   ❑
   (e) having a drink (i.e., beer,
       wine, liquor)   ❑   ❑   ❑
   (f) talking it over with friends
       and relatives   ❑   ❑   ❑

5. Have you ever gone to a doctor, psychologist,
   social worker, clergy, or other counsellor for help   Yes   No
   with an emotional problem?   ❑   ❑

6. How many cigarettes do you smoke a day?
   ❑ More than 2 packs   ❑ 1-2 packs   ❑ Less than 1 pack
   ❑ Do not smoke every day   ❑ Do not smoke at all

7. How often do you have a drink of wine, beer or another type of beverage containing alcohol?

- ❏ 3 or more times a day
- ❏ 2 times a day
- ❏ Daily or almost every day
- ❏ Once or twice a week
- ❏ Less than once a week
- ❏ Never

8. If you drink wine, beer or other beverages containing alcohol, how often do you have 1 or 2 drinks at a sitting?

❏ Almost always ❏ Often ❏ Sometimes ❏ Never

9. If you drink wine, beer or other beverages containing alcohol, how often do you have 4 or more drinks at a sitting?

❏ Almost always ❏ Often ❏ Sometimes ❏ Never

10. What prescribed medications do you take? *List all.* _____

11. What other medications and drugs do you use (including prescription, over-the-counter, off-the-shelf medications and illegal drugs)? *List all.* _____

12. Which, if any, of the following experiences are important to you as reasons for your drinking or taking other drugs (including tobacco)? *Check all that apply.*

- (a) It helps me forget my worries. ❏
- (b) It helps me feel better when I am not feeling well. ❏
- (c) It gives me relief when I am angry. ❏
- (d) It helps me when I am depressed or nervous. ❏

13. Which, if any, or the following experiences have you had in connection with drinking or using other drugs during the past year? *Check all that apply.*

- (a) taking a few quick drinks or using drugs before going to a party ❏
- (b) getting into a heated argument while drinking or taking drugs ❏
- (c) having trouble driving because of drinking or taking other drugs ❏

(d) feeling that your drinking or other drug use had
    a harmful effect on your home life   ❑

(e) starting to drink or take other drugs and finding
    it difficult to stop   ❑

(f) having friends or relatives worry or complain
    about your drinking or other drug use   ❑

(g) having a friend or relative tell you about things
    you said or did while your were drinking or taking
    other drugs and that you do not remember   ❑

(h) having a severe hangover or other drug effects
    (e.g., seeing or hearing things that were
    not really there)   ❑

	Yes	No
14. Have you ever decided to quit or cut down on your drinking or drug use (including tobacco), but then started up again?	❑	❑
15. Have you ever used any mood-altering drugs (e.g., for anxiety, for help sleeping, diet pills, cocaine) to such an extent that you felt you needed them?	❑	❑
16. Has your mother or father ever had problems with alcohol or other drugs (including tobacco)?	❑	❑

	Never Pregnant	Yes	No
17. Have there been times during pregnancy that you got intoxicated or very high from drinking alcohol or taking other drugs?	❑	❑	❑

Adapted from Blume & Russell.

TWEAK Screening Tool for Alcohol Use

The TWEAK test can be given to the client to fill out herself or it can be used as part of a routine history-taking.

TWEAK TEST

Do you drink alcoholic beverages? If you do, please take our "TWEAK Test."

T   **Tolerance:** How many drinks does it take to make you feel high? (Record number of drinks)   _____

W   **Worry:** Have close friends or relatives worried or complained about your drinking in the past year?   _____

E   **Eye-Opener:** Do you sometimes have a drink in the morning when you first get up?   _____

A   **Amnesia (Blackouts):** Has a friend or family member ever told you about things you said or did while you were drinking that you could not remember?   _____

K(C)   **Cut Down:** Do you sometimes feel the need to cut down on your drinking?   _____

Source: Russell et al. (1994).

---

*An **Important Note:** Especially when using the TWEAK questionnaire with women, the "E" or "Eye-Opener" question might provide more useful information if it were to read as follows: "Have you ever needed a drink or medication of some kind first thing in the morning to steady your nerves or get over a hangover?" [Blume, 1994]*

Scoring the TWEAK

The "tolerance" question scores *2 points* if a woman reports it takes 3 or more drinks to feel the effects of alcohol. The "worry" question scores *2 points* for a positive ("yes") response. Each of the last three questions scores *1 point* for a positive ("yes") response. A Total score of *2 or more points* indicates the woman is likely to have a drinking problem.

ICD-10 (International Classification of Diseases, 10th Edition)

The alcohol or drug dependence syndrome is a diagnostic category in ICD-10. In this official classification of disorders, dependence is diagnosed if a person qualifies on three of the six criteria. Below are a set of questions that ask directly about the constituents of the ICD-10 dependence syndrome, with a scoring procedure. You can use this as an indication of dependence, although only a qualified health professional should make a formal diagnosis. Dependence on one or more substances is one indication that a person has a problem with alcohol or other drug use. The ICD-10 can be used to measure dependence on a variety of different substances. For example, in the following questions you can substitute "alcohol," "pills to help you sleep," "cannabis," etc. for the word, "substance." Ask all 11 questions for each substance you are interested in knowing about.

ICD-10

During the past 12 months:

1. Strong urge to use

> 1. Have you felt a strong urge or desire to use the substance (e.g., alcohol, sleeping pills, cannabis)?

2. Difficult to control use

> 2a Have you started using the substance when you had decided not to use it?

> 2b Have you used the substance much more or for much longer than you intended?

> 2c Have you tried to stop or cut down but found that you could not?

3. Physiological withdrawal OR Use to relieve withdrawal

> 3a Have you felt sick or found yourself shaking when you cut down or stopped using the substance?

> 3b Have you taken the substance to get over any bad after-effects of the substance?

I C D - 1 0 *continued ...*

....

4. Tolerance

> 4. Have you found that your usual amount of the substance had much less effect on you than it once did?

5. Progressive neglect of other activities in favor of substance use

> 5a Have you given up or neglected pleasures or interests in favor of using the substance?
>
> 5b Have you spent a lot of time using the substance, on getting over its effects, or on doing things to get the substance?

6. Persistent use despite adverse physical or mental effects

> 6a Have you kept on using the substance even though you had a health problem caused or made worse by the substance?
>
> 6b Have you kept on using the substance even though it was making you depressed, uninterested in things, suspicious or distrustful?

Source: Paglia. (1995).

Scoring the ICD-10

A score is arrived at by assigning *1 point* for each *"yes"* answer, as follows:

Criteria 1	yes = 1
Criteria 2	yes to 2a or 2b or 2c = 1
Criteria 3	yes to 3a or 3b = 1
Criteria 4	yes = 1
Criteria 5	yes to 5a or 5b = 1
Criteria 6	yes to 6a or 6b = 1

The lowest score possible is 0 and the highest 6. A total score of *3 or more* suggests the person is dependent on the particular substance asked about.

REFERENCES

Addiction Research Foundation. (1994). *Alcohol and Drug Treatment in Ontario: A Guide for Helping Professionals.* Toronto: Addiction Research Foundation, v, 44.

Addiction Research Foundation. (1995). *LINK — Violence Against Women and Children in Relationships and the Use of Alcohol and Drugs: Searching for Solutions.* An Educational Package. Toronto: Addiction Research Foundation.

Addiction Research Foundation & Health Canada. (1991). *Youth & Drugs: An Educational Package for Professionals.* Ottawa: Supply and Services Canada.

Ashley, Mary Jane, Ferrence, Roberta, Room, Robin, Single, Eric, Bondy, Susan & Rehm, Jurgen. (In Press). Moderate Drinking and Health: Implications of Recent Evidence for Clinical Practice. *Canadian Family Physician.*

Beckman, Linda J. (1994). Treatment Needs of Women With Alcohol Problems. *Alcohol Health & Research World*, 18(3):206-211.

Beckman, Linda J. (1984). Treatment Needs of Women Alcoholics. *Alcoholism Treatment Quarterly*, 1(2):101-114.

Beckman, Linda J. & Kocel, Katherine M. (1982). The Treatment-Delivery System and Alcohol Abuse in Women: Social policy implications. *Journal of Social Issues*, 38(2):139-151.

Blume, Sheila B. (1994). Women and Addictive Disorders. *American Society of Addiction Medicine.* 1-16.

Blume, Sheila B. (1992). Alcohol and other drug problems in women. In Lowinson, Joyce H., Ruiz, Pedro, Millman, Robert B. & Langrod, John G. (eds.). *Substance Abuse: A Comprehensive Textbook.* Baltimore: Williams & Wilkins, 794-807.

Blume, Sheila B. & Russell, Marcia. *Women's Health and Drug Use Questionnaire.* Personal Communication.

Bullock, Doug. (1993). The physically disabled substance abuser. In Howard, Betty-Anne M., Harrison, Susan, Carver, Virginia & Lightfoot, Lynn (eds.). *Alcohol & Drug Problems: A Practical Guide for Counsellors.* Toronto: Addiction Research Foundation, 219-228.

Center for Substance Abuse Treatment. (1994). *Practical Approaches in the Treatment of Women who Abuse Alcohol and Other Drugs.* Rockville, MD: U.S. Department of Health and Human Services, 275.

Finkelstein, Norma, Duncan, Sally Anne, Derman, Laura & Smeltz, Janet. (1990). *Getting Sober, Getting Well: A Treatment Guide for Caregivers who Work with Women.* Cambridge, MA: Women's Alcoholism Program of CASPAR, xiii, 632.

Galbraith, Susan. (1991). Women and legal drugs. In Roth, Paula (ed.). *Alcohol and Drugs are Women's Issues.* Volume One: A Review of the Issues. Metuchen, NJ: Women's Action Alliance and Scarecrow Press, 150-154.

Harris, Nanci. (May, 1994). *Women's Use & Misuse of Alcohol and Other Drugs: Understanding the Issues.* Presentation.

Harrison, Susan. (1993). Working with women. In Howard, Betty-Anne M., Harrison, Susan, Carver, Virginia & Lightfoot, Lynn (eds.). *Alcohol & Drug Problems: A Practical Guide for Counsellors.* Toronto: Addiction Research Foundation, 195-218.

Infant Mental Health Promotion Project & Metro Toronto Addiction Treatment Services Committee. (No date). *Pregnancy & Alcohol/Drug Use: A Professional's Guide to Identification and Care of Mother and Infant.* Pamphlet.

Miller, William R. & Rollnick, Stephen. (1991). *Motivational Interviewing: Preparing People to Change Addictive Behavior.* New York: Guilford, xvii, 348.

Ontario Ministry of Health. (1988). *A Framework for the Response to Alcohol and Drug Problems in Ontario.* Toronto: Ontario Ministry of Health, 62.

Paglia, Angela. (1995). *Alcohol, Tobacco, and Drugs: Dependence, Problems, and Consequences of Use.* A Report of the 1994 Ontario Alcohol and Other Drug Opinion Survey. Toronto: Addiction Research Foundation, Document No. 121.

Prochaska, James O., Norcross, John C. & DiClemente, Carlo C. (1994). *Changing for Good.* New York: William Morrow, 304.

Reed, Beth Glover. (1991). Linkages: Battering, sexual assault, incest, child sexual abuse, teen pregnancy, dropping out of school and the alcohol and drug connection. In Roth, Paula (ed.). *Alcohol and Drugs are Women's Issues.* Volume One: A Review of the Issues. Metuchen, NJ: Women's Action Alliance and Scarecrow Press, 130-149.

Reed, Beth Glover. (1985). Drug Misuse and Dependency in Women: The Meaning and Implications of Being Considered a Special population or Minority Group. *The International Journal of the Addictions*, 20(1):13-62.

Russell, Marcia, Martier, Susan S., Sokol, Robert J., Mudar, Pamela, Bottoms, Sidney, Jacobson, Sandra & Jacobson, Joseph. (1994). Screening for Pregnancy Risk-Drinking. *Alcoholism: Clinical and Experimental Research*, 18(5):1156-1161.

Sanchez-Craig, Martha. (1995). *Saying When: How to Quit Drinking or Cut Down.* 2nd Ed. (Revised),Toronto: Addiction Research Foundation, 82.

Women and Wellness

HEALTH PROMOTION ISSUES

What Is Health Promotion?

Health promotion is defined as "a process of enabling people to increase control over, and improve their health." *[World Health Organization, 1986]*

Health promotion focuses on promoting good health rather than on providing treatment. It is a holistic approach to health that includes, but is not restricted to, prevention strategies.

Health promotion is based on the premise that an individual's state of health is influenced by three major factors:
- her environment
- her lifestyle
- her personal characteristics (e.g., physical and personality traits she is born with or acquires)

Everyone can benefit from health promotion — whether they are currently in good health or have health-related problems (e.g., with alcohol or other drugs).

Health promotion has three major purposes:
- health enhancement — to increase vitality and good health in all people
- risk avoidance — to ensure that people at low risk of developing health-related problems stay that way

- risk reduction — to change or modify environmental conditions, behaviors or predisposing characteristics that put people at risk for developing health-related problems

As a counsellor working with women, you may have the opportunity to use health promotion strategies with individuals or groups of clients. You may also have the opportunity to get involved in health promotion projects in your community. Such projects might be initiated by a local Community Health Centre, Public Health Department, or by government.

Putting Health Promotion Strategies into Action

There are five health promotion strategies you can use to promote the health of people living in your communities or working with your agencies. These health promotion strategies share some common features. To be most effective, they should be used in combination with each other.

Advocacy

Individuals and groups can put pressure on those with power (at local, provincial or federal levels) to address important issues. For example, you can:

- lobby for healthier environments, healthy public policy, and a reduction in barriers to access health and health-related services
- encourage women who have concerns to take action toward making social change; issues may include policies affecting equity, social justice, targeted advertising of tobacco or alcohol to women, images of women in the media, access to health care, poverty, access to day care, personal safety, neighborhood drug trafficking, etc.
- inform women of any existing groups with whom they have a common concern or of upcoming community actions or demonstrations related to their concern

Community Development

Work toward enabling communities to understand and control the circumstances that limit access to good health. For example, you can:

- help bring together a group of women to work toward a shared objective (e.g., community garden, community kitchen, neighbourhood watch); such a task helps build self-esteem and self-efficacy, and provides social support and a sense of accomplishment

Social Support

Supportive social relationships and social networks are key factors in helping women cope with stress and feelings of isolation. For example, you can:

- assist in connecting women who have similar interests or experiences
- inform clients about support, self-help, interest groups or clubs in your community that they may be interested in

Health Education

Provide knowledge and teaching skills to address health concerns. For example, you can:

- provide women with information they need to make informed decisions about their health, use of substances and alternatives to use, etc.
- provide information to women verbally, on handouts or pamphlets, on videos or audio tapes, to groups at workshops, or you can refer women to other organizations that can give them more detailed information

Social Marketing

Use marketing for communicating a message or idea to raise awareness about an issue or to influence attitudes about a behavior. For example, you can:

- get involved with a community action group such as a Drug Awareness Week committee and encourage the group to consider issues of concern to women
- put up posters in your office to raise awareness about issues, community groups and services related to substance use and/or of interest to women

Health promotion is not just about personal change. It is also about changing societal attitudes and the social environment in which we live.
- it is fine to tell a woman to use medication only when absolutely necessary — but it is easier for her to follow this guideline if her doctor and drug advertisements give her the same message and if she has other realistic alternatives

All women do not have the same choices in life.
- women choose from among the choices available to them — an endless number of factors can influence or limit their choices
- women have differing financial resources, social supports, cultural backgrounds, and so on — these influence a woman's ability to engage in activities that cost money, to have time for herself, to get someone to look after her children, to buy and cook healthy foods, to assert herself in a relationship where she may find the consequences too severe (e.g., partner may abuse or leave her, employer might fire her)

It is important to consider these issues when advising women on how to make healthier choices in their lives. Otherwise, advice could become an additional burden that women have to deal with.

HEALTHY ALTERNATIVES TO UNHEALTHY SUBSTANCE USE

Counsellors can support women by providing them with information and suggestions about leading healthy lives. This can include alternative coping strategies to alcohol and drug use. Finding the right combination of activities or approaches that work for her will help a woman take more control of her life and will benefit her overall health and well-being. The more coping strategies she has available to her, the better.

It is important to explore with each woman what activities she has found relaxing or rewarding in the past or which new activities she thinks she would like to try now. The most important thing is for a woman to enjoy what she is doing rather than to strive for perfection.

144.

It is important for a woman to find the right balance in whatever she does. As with alcohol and other drug use, alternatives can become compulsions. Instead of confronting the real issues in her life, a woman might keep her mind and body busy with schedules and details. For example, she might have a rigid exercise routine that she insists on following every day — even though she may have something more important to do or there may be times when she prefers to simply go for a walk, read a book, or do nothing.

Practical Suggestions for Women

Taking care of herself is of utmost importance if a woman is to stay physically, mentally, emotionally and spiritually healthy. But changes should be undertaken slowly so that a woman does not feel so over-whelmed that she reverts to negative patterns or feels like a failure for not reaching her planned goals.

The following suggestions are things that a woman can do to enhance her overall health and sense of well-being. As a counsel-lor, you can help her set realistic goals (in small steps) and be supportive of her efforts to achieve them.

Take care of her own needs.
- find a balance between taking care of her own needs and the needs of others — taking time for herself gives a woman strength

Accept that stress is a natural reaction to life events.
- stress is the body's normal response to any change — the more changes, the more stress
- the response to the change (stressor) can be positive (effective coping) or negative (ineffective coping)
- it is important that a woman develop effective stress management or coping techniques suited to her individual characteristics and lifestyle

Be more assertive — but only if it is safe to do so.
- express her opinions and do the things she wants to do
- say "no" to things she does not want to do or does not have time for — a woman may find it difficult to change her behav-

ior in this way, but if she starts by saying "no" to small things this will give her the practice and confidence to say "no" to bigger things
- ask questions of her doctor and play an active role in the type of health care she receives

Increase her support network.
- keep in touch — call a friend, talk to a neighbor
- find and spend time with people she likes and trusts
- join a group around an issue she is interested in, attend community workshops (many are free)

Have healthy eating habits.
- eat regular, well-balanced meals:
    - eat plenty of fresh fruits and vegetables, legumes and whole grains (bread, rice, pasta)
    - avoid too much fat in her diet by eating lean meat, poultry, fish and low-fat dairy products
    - cut down on sugar, salt and caffeine
- get nutritional information and counselling at local hospitals (cost is covered by provincial health plans) and possibly other health care centres

Engage in leisure activities.
- choose healthy activities: listen to music, swim, walk, sing, volunteer, play a sport, walk the dog, spend time in the garden, play a game, cook or bake, read, paint, weave, knit, watch television, play cards, go to the library, have a bubble bath
- develop new hobbies and interests

Get involved in her community.

Exercise regularly.
- increase her activity level and enjoyment of life
- set reasonable goals when beginning an exercise program — a woman needs to consider which activities she likes, how much time she has, and how easy it is for her to do a particular activity

146.

- exercise where it is convenient and within her budget — at home (self-directed or with a videotape), at a community centre, at the Y (subsidized memberships are available)
- exercise can also include activities such as walking the dog, gardening

Take a break.
- relax where she is (at work, on the bus), close her eyes, and imagine herself in a peaceful, pleasant setting
- go out for a walk, watch a movie, chat with a friend, listen to music, enjoy a good laugh, or just do nothing

Use relaxation techniques.
- these can range from a minute or two of stretching, deep breathing, imagining pleasant situations and feelings, or walking around to longer and regular practise of yoga, meditation, muscle relaxation, or getting a massage
- do slow, deep breathing — get comfortable, inhale slowly and deeply through her nose, hold her breath for a few seconds, and then exhale slowly; repeat this pattern three or four times in each session; do this a few times a day or whenever she feels her stress level getting too high
- do progressive muscle relaxation — starting at the top of her body, tense a muscle, hold the tension for five to 10 seconds, and notice how it feels; relax the tension for about 20 seconds and enjoy the relaxed feeling; continue this way from her head to her toes, tensing and relaxing one muscle or set of muscles at a time
- listen to relaxation tapes

Keep a journal.
- write down her thoughts and feelings

Create an activity calendar to plan and organize things to do, to keep track of appointments.

Get enough sleep and rest.

Have a good professional relationship with her doctor or other health care provider.
- find a doctor she can talk openly with, who discusses options with her
- a woman is an equal partner in deciding the type of health care she receives — it is okay for her to question diagnoses and suggested solutions (medication, surgery), and to get a second opinion if she chooses

Have regular checkups with her doctor and dentist.

Work with a counsellor.

Alternatives to Non-Essential Medication

Many people, especially women, may take medication for a variety of ailments because they may not be aware of non-drug alternatives. Alternative options can reduce or eliminate some unpleasant symptoms (e.g., insomnia, anxiety, fatigue) without the use of drugs.

Some doctors suggest or prescribe medication even though non-medical solutions:
- are healthier
- are just as effective for relieving symptoms
- reinforce positive coping skills
- teach people how to get rid of symptoms rather than simply cover them up
- have no side effects
- do not lead to dependence

- Some women may benefit from, and may prefer, alternative therapies such as massage, chiropractic, and acupuncture. In deciding which type of therapy to pursue and who to go to for help, it would be best for women to:
  - educate themselves about the benefits and possible negative effects of each procedure
  - make sure the therapist is a licensed practitioner
  - get a referral —from friends, doctor, etc.

148.

EXAMPLES OF ALTERNATIVES

For sleep problems:
- get fresh air and exercise during the day
- decrease caffeine intake (coffee, tea, cola drinks, chocolate) during the day and do not have any at night; instead, drink hot milk, hot water, or herbal tea without caffeine
- try not to smoke before bedtime
- soak in a warm bath
- practise relaxation techniques
- read a book or magazine — one that does not upset or scare her
- if her thoughts are keeping her awake, she should write them down and put them aside until the next day

For anxiety and stress:
- understand that some anxiety and stress is normal
- get counselling and support — talk things over with family, friends, or someone else she trusts
- say "no" to things she does not want to do
- consider her own needs first instead of always taking care of everyone else
- exercise
- relax with a good book or soothing music

149.

A WOMAN'S HEALTH BILL OF RIGHTS AND RESPONSIBILITIES

1. I have a right to be treated as an equal human being.

2. I have a right to be listened to and have my problems taken seriously.

3. I have a right to an explanation that I can understand in my native language (using a translator if necessary) of any questions concerning my health care.

4. I have a right to know the choices I face in getting treated for any health problem, and to have the possible side effects of any drugs or surgical treatments clearly explained.

5. I have a right to choose the types of treatment I prefer from among the options offered to me by my doctor.

6. I have a right for normal events in my life, such as pregnancy and menopause, not to be treated as diseases requiring treatment.

7. I have a right to choose natural therapies and not be ridiculed for doing so.

8. I have a right to request a second opinion on any major surgery or health decision.

9. I have a right to refuse any drug or surgical treatment.

10. I have a responsibility to become knowledgeable about my body and how it works.

11. I have a responsibility to learn as much as possible about my health problems so I can make informed choices.

12. I have a responsibility to look after my diet, reduce stress, exercise and relax on a regular basis.

13. I have the responsibility to avoid pressuring my doctor into giving me drugs when I don't need them.

14. I have a responsibility to prepare my questions for my doctor beforehand and schedule adequate appointment time to discuss them.

15. I am ultimately responsible for my own health care, using my doctor as a resource rather than an authority.

Source: DeMarco. (1995).

REFERENCES

Action on Women's Addictions — Research & Education (AWARE). (1995). *Making Connections: A Booklet about Women and Prescription Drugs and Alcohol.* Kingston, ON: AWARE, 34.

DeMarco, Carolyn. (1995). *Take Charge of Your Body: A Woman's Guide to Health.* Revised Edition. Winlaw, BC: Well Woman.

Finkelstein, Norma, Duncan, Sally Anne, Derman, Laura & Smeltz, Janet. (1990). *Getting Sober, Getting Well: A Treatment Guide for Caregivers who Work with Women.* Cambridge, MA: Women's Alcoholism Program of CASPAR, xiii, 632.

Health Canada. (1992). *Heart Health Equality: Mobilizing Communities for Action.* Ottawa: Supply and Services Canada, 24.

Ontario Ministry of Health. (1991). *Action: A Guide for Community Health Promotion Planning.* Toronto: Queen's Printer for Ontario, vi, 20.

Premier's Council on Health, Well-being and Social Justice. (1993). *Nurturing Health.* Toronto: Queen's Printer for Ontario, 24.

Facts about Alcohol and Other Drugs

ALCOHOL

Drug Class: Sedative/Hypnotic

Synopsis

Alcohol is often not thought of as a drug – largely because its use is common for both religious and social purposes in most parts of the world. It is a drug, however, and compulsive drinking in excess has become one of modern society's most serious problems.

Beverage alcohol (scientifically known as ethyl alcohol, or ethanol) is produced by fermenting or distilling various fruits, vegetables, or grains. Ethyl alcohol itself is a clear, colorless liquid. Alcoholic beverages get their distinctive colors from the diluents, additives, and by-products of fermentation.

In Ontario, beer is fermented to contain about 5% alcohol by volume (or 3.5% in light beer). Most wine is fermented to have between 10% and 14% alcohol content; however, such fortified wines as sherry, port, and vermouth contain between 14% and 20%. Distilled spirits (whisky, vodka, rum, gin) are first fermented, then distilled to raise the alcohol content. In Canada, the concentration of alcohol in spirits is 40% by volume. Some liqueurs may be stronger.

The effects of drinking do not depend on the type of alcoholic beverage – but rather on the amount of alcohol consumed on a specific occasion. The following table outlines the alcohol content of

153.

various beverages. The right-hand column shows the amount of alcohol consumed in each drink.

How Alcohol Works

Alcohol– is rapidly absorbed into the bloodstream from the small intestine, and less rapidly from the stomach and colon. In proportion to its concentration in the bloodstream, alcohol decreases activity in parts of the brain and spinal cord. The drinker's blood alcohol concentration depends on:
- the amount consumed in a given time
- the drinker's size, sex, body build, and metabolism
- the type and amount of food in the stomach.

Once the alcohol has passed into the blood, however, no food or beverage can retard or interfere with its effects. Fruit sugar, however, in some cases can shorten the duration of alcohol's effect by speeding up its elimination from the blood.

In the average adult, the rate of metabolism is about 8.5 g of alcohol per hour (i.e. about two-thirds of a regular beer or about 30 mL of spirits an hour). This rate can vary dramatically among individuals, however, depending on such diverse factors as usual amount of drinking, physique, sex, liver size, and genetic factors.

Effects

The effects of any drug depend on several factors:
- the amount taken at one time
- the user's past drug experience
- the manner in which the drug is taken
- the circumstances under which the drug is taken (the place, the user's psychological and emotional stability, the presence of other people, the concurrent use of other drugs, etc.).

It is the amount of alcohol in the blood that causes the effects. In the following table, the left-hand column lists the number of milligrams of alcohol in each decilitre of blood, that is, the blood alcohol concentration, or BAC. (For example, an average person may get a blood alcohol concentration of 50 mg/dL after two drinks consumed quickly.) The right-hand column describes the usual effects

154.

of these amounts on normal people – those who haven't developed a tolerance to alcohol.

BAC (ma/dL) Effect

50 Mild intoxication
Feeling of warmth, skin flushed; impaired judgment; decreased inhibitions

100 Obvious intoxication in most people
Increased impairment of judgment, inhibition, attention, and control; Some impairment of muscular performance; slowing of reflexes

150 Obvious intoxication in all normal people
Staggering gait and other muscular incoordination; slurred speech; double vision; memory and comprehension loss

250 Extreme intoxication or stupor
Reduced response to stimuli; inability to stand; vomiting; incontinence; sleepiness

350 Coma
Unconsciousness; little response to stimuli; incontinence; low body temperature; poor respiration; fall in blood pressure; clammy skin

500 Death likely

Drinking heavily over a short period of time usually results in a "hangover" - headache, nausea, shakiness, and sometimes vomiting, beginning from 8 to 12 hours later. A hangover is due partly to poisoning by alcohol and other components of the drink, and partly to the body's reaction to withdrawal from alcohol. Although there are dozens of home remedies suggested for hangovers, there is currently no known effective cure.

Combining alcohol with other drugs can make the effects of these other drugs much stronger and more dangerous. Many accidental deaths have occurred after people have used alcohol combined with other drugs. Cannabis, tranquillizers, barbiturates and other sleeping pills, or antihistamines (in cold, cough, and allergy remedies) should not be taken with alcohol. Even a small amount of alcohol with any of these drugs can seriously impair a person's ability to drive a car, for example.

Long-term effects of alcohol appear after repeated use over a period of many months or years. The negative physical and psychological effects of chronic abuse are numerous; some are potentially life-threatening.

Some of these harmful consequences are primary – that is, they result directly from prolonged exposure to alcohol's toxic effects (such as heart and liver disease or inflammation of the stomach).

Others are secondary; indirectly related to chronic alcohol abuse, they include loss of appetite, vitamin deficiencies, infections, and sexual impotence or menstrual irregularities.

The risk of serious disease increases with the amount of alcohol consumed. Early death rates are much higher for heavy drinkers than for light drinkers or abstainers, particularly from heart and liver disease, pneumonia, some types of cancer, acute alcohol poisoning, accident, homicide, and suicide. No precise limits of safe drinking can be recommended.

According to 1988 figures from Statistics Canada, 2,828 deaths were directly attributable to alcohol in that year. There were, however, an estimated 13,870 more deaths – five times as many – indirectly caused by alcohol.

Tolerance and Dependence

People who drink on a regular basis become tolerant to many of the unpleasant effects of alcohol, and thus are able to drink more before suffering these effects. Yet even with increased consumption, many such drinkers don't appear intoxicated. Because they continue to work and socialize reasonably well, their deteriorating physical condition may go unrecognized by others until severe damage develops – or until they are hospitalized for other reasons and suddenly experience alcohol withdrawal symptoms.

Psychological dependence on alcohol may occur with regular use of even relatively moderate daily amounts. It may also occur in people who consume alcohol only under certain conditions, such as before and during social occasions. This form of dependence refers to a craving for alcohol's psychological effects, although not necessarily in amounts that produce serious intoxication. For psychologically dependent drinkers, the lack of alcohol tends to make them anxious and, in some cases, panicky.

Physical dependence occurs in consistently heavy drinkers. Since their bodies have adapted to the presence of alcohol, they suffer withdrawal symptoms if they suddenly stop drinking. Withdrawal symptoms range from jumpiness, sleeplessness, sweating, and poor appetite, to tremors (the "shakes"), convulsions, hallucinations, and sometimes death.

Alcohol and Pregnancy
Pregnant women who drink risk having babies with fetal alcohol effects (known as fetal alcohol syndrome or FAS). The most serious of these effects include mental retardation, growth deficiency, head and facial deformities, joint and limb abnormalities, and heart defects. While it is known that the risk of bearing an FAS-afflicted child increases with the amount of alcohol consumed, a safe level of consumption has not been determined.

Who Uses Alcohol?
In a 1990 nation-wide Gallup poll, 79% of adults reported they had at some point drunk alcohol. A 1989 survey of adults in Ontario found that 83% reported ever having used alcohol, with 55% saying they have five drinks or more at a single sitting and 10% reporting daily drinking.

Among young people between 12 and 19 years, a 1985 national survey recorded 73% using alcohol at least once in the past year. Of Ontario students in grades 7, 9, 11, and 13 polled in 1989, 66% admitted to alcohol use, with more than 80% of the grade 11 and 13 students saying they drank. More than one in five of all those who drank said they did so more than once a week. Since the legal drinking age in Ontario is 19, it appears that alcohol has a high degree of social acceptance, whether legal or not.

Total alcohol consumption in Canada during 1988/89 reached 202.9 million litres. This corresponds to an average annual consump-

157.

tion of 9.9 L of alcohol for each Canadian over the age of 15 – that is, about 11 drinks per week or a little under two drinks a day. Beer, making up 52% of the total volume, was the most popular drink, with spirits in second place at 31%, and wine a distant third at 17%.

In recent years, Canadians have spent about $9.6 billion a year for alcohol in retail stores and another estimated $2.6 billion for alcohol consumed in taverns and restaurants.

There is a direct relationship between the overall level of consumption within a population and the number of alcohol-dependent people. A nation with a low per-capita consumption rate has a lower number of heavy users, whereas one with widespread use and high per-capita consumption has a proportionately higher rate of alcohol-related diseases and deaths.

Most researchers agree that one in 20 drinkers in North America has an alcohol dependency problem.

Alcohol and the Law

Alcohol legislation is a joint responsibility of the federal and provincial governments, and many laws regulate its manufacture, distribution, advertising, possession, and consumption.

In Ontario, marketing and consumption of alcohol is primarily governed by the provincial *Liquor Licence Act.* It is an offence for anyone under 19 years to possess, consume, or purchase alcohol. It is also illegal to sell or supply alcohol to anyone known to be or appearing to be (unless that person has proof otherwise) under the age of 19. It is not illegal, though, for parents or guardians to give an under-age child a drink at home. Provisions similar to Ontario's apply in most other Canadian provinces and in the Yukon and Northwest Territories, as well as in many states in the United States.

The Act also makes it illegal to sell or supply alcohol to a person who appears to be intoxicated.

As well, anyone who sells or supplies alcohol to others - whether these are patrons of a tavern or restaurant or guests in a private home – may be held civilly liable if intoxicated patrons or guests injure themselves or others.

The federal criminal law sets out a range of drinking and driving offences. It is illegal, for example, to operate a motor vehicle, boat, or aircraft while impaired by any amount of alcohol or other drugs. The manner in which one drives, slurred speech or physical incoordination, and the smell of alcohol may all be used as evidence of a person's impairment.

It is also a criminal offence to drive with a blood alcohol concentration (BAC) above .08% (which means with more than 80 mg of alcohol in each 100 mL of blood in one's bloodstream)

The *Criminal Code* sets out complex provisions authorizing police to demand breath samples or, in limited circumstances, blood samples, from suspected drinking drivers. Those refusing to comply can be convicted unless they have a reasonable excuse.

The *Ontario Highway Traffic Act* gives police broad powers to stop drivers to determine if they have been drinking and to issue a 12-hour licence suspension if their BAC is above .05% (i.e., higher than 50 mg of alcohol per 100 mL of blood).

Drinking and driving is by far the largest criminal cause of death and injury in Canada. In 1988, there were 121,307 Canadians charged with federal drinking and driving offences: 110,773 for impaired operation of a motor vehicle; 1,194 for impaired operation causing bodily harm; and 158 for causing death. Another 8,786 people were charged for failure or refusal to provide a breath sample for testing. In all, 19,808 Canadians were jailed for drinking and driving offences in 1988/89.

Source: Addiction Research Foundation (1991).

AMPHETAMINES

Drug Class: Central Nervous System Stimulants

Synopsis

Amphetamines and amphetamine-related drugs are central nervous system stimulants whose actions resemble those of adrenaline, one of the body's natural hormones.

The most important of these stimulants are the original drug, amphetamine, and its close chemical relations, methamphetamine and dextroamphetamine. Only the latter, under the trade name Dexedrine, is legally manufactured in Canada today. Everything else is synthesized in illicit "basement" laboratories.

159.

Amphetamine was first introduced in the 1930s as a remedy for nasal congestion. Later, all three drugs were found to be effective in treating such other conditions as hyperactivity in children and narcolepsy (uncontrollable sleeping fits). Although they were also prescribed to control obesity and depression, their use for these disorders has been discontinued because patients became quickly and seriously dependent.

The amphetamines have long been taken for their stimulant and euphoric effects. When they were easily available in Canada, truck drivers, students, and athletes were among those who used them extensively to prolong their normal periods of wakefulness and endurance.

Among street drug users, injectable methamphetamine, usually called "speed," has been the most popular of this group of drugs because the "high" is more rapid and intense than when the drug is taken orally. There are now reports of a smokable form of methamphetamine, known on the street as "ice."

Other street names for these drugs are bennies, glass, crystal, crank, pep pills, and uppers.

Amphetamine misuse has declined dramatically since the near epidemic between 1950 and 1970. At the same time, however, there has been a marked increase in the use of such other stimulants as cocaine. As well, drugs related to amphetamine – such as MDA, PMA, TMA, and STP – have appeared on the street.
(See sections on Cocaine and Hallucinogens.)

Appearance

Illicit amphetamine appears as crystals, chunks, and fine to coarse powders, off-white to yellow in color, and supplied loose (in plastic or foil bags) or in capsules or tablets of various sizes and colors. The drug may be sniffed, smoked, injected, or taken orally in tablet or capsule form.

Effects

The effects of any drug depend on several factors:
- the amount taken at one time
- the user's past drug experience
- the manner in which the drug is taken

• the circumstances under which the drug is taken (the place, the user's psychological and emotional stability, the presence of other people, the simultaneous use of alcohol or other drugs, etc.).

Amphetamines, like adrenaline, affect not only the brain but also the heart, lungs, and many other organs. Short-term effects appear soon after a single dose and disappear within a few hours or days.

At low doses, such as those prescribed medically, physical effects include loss of appetite, rapid breathing and heartbeat, high blood pressure, and dilated pupils. Larger doses may produce fever, sweating, headache, blurred vision, and dizziness. And very high doses may cause flushing, pallor, very rapid or irregular heartbeat, tremors, loss of coordination, and collapse. Deaths have been reported as a direct result of amphetamine use. Some have occurred as a consequence of burst blood vessels in the brain, heart failure, or very high fever.

The psychological effects of short-term use include a feeling of well-being and great alertness and energy. With increased doses, users may become talkative, restless, and excited, and may feel a sense of power and superiority. They may also behave in a bizarre, repetitive fashion. Many become hostile and aggressive. Paradoxically, in children these drugs frequently produce a calming effect and are often prescribed for hyperactivity.

Long-term effects appear soon after repeated use over a long period. With prolonged amphetamine use, the short-term effects are exaggerated. Because amphetamines specifically suppress appetite, chronic heavy users generally fail to eat properly and thus develop various illnesses related to vitamin deficiencies and malnutrition.

Users may also be more prone to illness because they are generally run down, lack sleep, and live in an unhealthy environment. Chronic heavy users may also develop amphetamine psychosis – a mental disturbance very similar to paranoid schizophrenia. The psychosis condition is an exaggeration of the short-term effects of high doses; the symptoms usually disappear within a few days or weeks after drug use is stopped.

Heavy users of amphetamines may be prone to sudden, violent, and irrational acts. These result from drug-induced self-centredness, distortions of perception, and delusions that other people are

161.

threatening or persecuting them. The deviant lifestyle of many users may increase the likelihood of such behavior.

In one Canadian study, violence (either accidental, self-inflicted, or perpetrated by others) was the leading cause of amphetamine-related deaths. Violent death was at least four times as common among regular users of amphetamines as among non-users of the same age and sex.

As a way of coping with undesired amphetamine effects, users may turn to other dependence-producing drugs. Depressant drugs, particularly barbiturates, alcohol, and opiates, may be used to aid sleep or compensate for overdose. Thus users risk, in turn, addiction to these drugs as well.

Infections from unsterile needles are not unusual among users who inject the drug. Some infections are passed from user to user via shared needles. Hepatitis, for example, is common among speed users who regularly employ a needle; AIDS (acquired immune deficiency syndrome) may spread in the same way.

Amphetamine products often contain substances that do not easily dissolve in water. When users inject the drug, these particles can pass into the body and block small blood vessels or weaken the blood vessel walls. Kidney damage, lung problems, strokes, or other tissue injury may result.

Tolerance and Dependence

Regular use of amphetamines induces tolerance to some effects, which means that more and more of the drug is required to produce the desired effects. Tolerance does not develop to all effects at the same rate, however; indeed, there may be increased sensitivity to some of them.

Chronic users may also become psychologically dependent on amphetamines. Psychological dependence exists when a drug is so central to a person's thoughts, emotions, and activities that the need to continue its use becomes a craving or compulsion. Experiments have shown that animals, when given a free choice, will readily operate pumps that inject them with cocaine or amphetamine. Animals dependent on amphetamines will work hard to get more of the drug.

Physical dependence occurs when the body has adapted to the presence of the drug, and withdrawal symptoms occur if its use is stopped abruptly. The most common symptoms of withdrawal among heavy amphetamine users are fatigue, long but troubled sleep, irritability, intense hunger, and moderate to severe depression, which may lead to suicidal behavior. Fits of violence may also occur. These disturbances can be temporarily reversed if the drug is taken again.

Amphetamines and Pregnancy

Little research has been done in humans into the effects of amphetamine use on pregnancy and fetal growth. Experiments with animals suggest, however, that use during pregnancy may produce adverse behavioral effects, such as hyperexcitability, in offspring. And among humans, several cases have been documented of withdrawal symptoms among newborn infants of mothers using amphetamines.

Other Stimulants

In the past few years, there has been increasing use of nasal decongestants for their relatively mild stimulant properties. Various combinations of ephedrine, phenylpropanolamine (PPA), and caffeine are often misrepresented as "speed" or are sold in capsules that resemble those of legally manufactured amphetamines; these are called "look-alike" stimulants. Taken in doses high enough to stimulate the central nervous system, these drugs (especially when used in combinations) can produce such side effects as high blood pressure, irregular heartbeat, and agitation. Deaths due to stroke have been reported following massive doses of look-alike combinations or of a related decongestant, propylhexadrine.

Who Uses Stimulants?

In the past, amphetamines were widely used medically to treat depression, obesity, and a variety of other conditions. Stringent government controls, however, have restricted their medical use in Canada to a small number of conditions, including Parkinson's disease, narcolepsy, and attention deficit disorder (hyperactivity) in children. Other drugs with similar chemical structures and effects – but said by their manufacturers to be different from amphetamines – have some popularity as appetite suppressants.

A 1989 Addiction Research Foundation survey of Ontario students in grades 7 to 13 found that 6.5% reported non-medical use

163.

of stimulants (other than cocaine) at least once during the preceding year. Among students aged 16 and 17, the rate of use was higher at 9%. It is believed that many of these students were consuming caffeine, ephedrine, and PPA in the form of amphetamine look-alikes or caffeine in over-the-counter stimulants.

Stimulants and the Law

Amphetamines are controlled drugs under Schedule G of Canada's *Food and Drugs Act* and are legally available only on prescription. Diethylpropion, an amphetamine-like drug contained in diet pills (e.g., Tenuate), became a controlled drug in 1978 after reports of mounting abuse. All drugs listed under Schedule G are restricted at the manufacturing and distribution stages. Anyone convicted of trafficking in these drugs or possessing them for the purpose of trafficking is guilty of an offence that, if tried by indictment, carries a maximum penalty of 10 years imprisonment.

Ephedrine and PPA are listed under Schedule C of the Food and Drugs Act, and are thus available in combination products without prescription.

It is illegal to obtain a prescription for amphetamines or any other controlled drug from health care professionals without notifying them that you have obtained a similar prescription through another practitioner within the preceding 30 days. Possessing amphetamines or other controlled drugs does not constitute an offence.

Source: Addiction Research Foundation (1991).

ANTIDEPRESSANTS

This type of medication is used to treat symptoms of depression. Depression is an illness that goes beyond feeling sad or unhappy. The symptoms may include sleep and appetite difficulties, low sex drive, poor concentration, lowered self esteem, and a sense of hopelessness. Usually several symptoms must be experienced before your physician will diagnose a major depression. These symptoms usually last for more than one week.

One approach to treating depression is to use medications called antidepressants. It is believed that one way antidepressants may act is by changing the levels of certain chemicals in the brain that affect our mood. They may take from a few days to four weeks to start having an effect on your mood, so time is required to give the medication a chance to be effective. Signs of improvement might include improved appetite, better sleep, and increased energy. Even though the medication takes a while to work, there is a high likelihood of success. It is very important to continue taking the medication on a regular basis and not to change how it is taken without consulting your doctor. It is usually necessary to take the medication for at least six months or longer.

If you experience any unusual symptoms while taking this medication, you should discuss these with your physician.

1. Always take this medication as prescribed by your physician.
2. It is very important that you take this medication regularly and do not miss any doses. It may take a few days to several weeks for the full benefits to be noticed. Do not stop taking the medication when you first start feeling better.
3. This medication may impair the mental and physical abilities required for driving a car or operating other machinery.
4. When combined with alcohol, you may feel more sleepy, dizzy, and lightheaded.
5. This medication may interact with other medications purchased over-the-counter in a pharmacy, or with those prescribed by a physician or dentist. Therefore, it is important to inform any physician or dentist you are receiving treatment from that you are taking this medication. Consult with your pharmacist before buying over-the-counter medications.
6. It is very important that your physician knows if you have been taking another antidepressant before starting this medication. Inform him or her if so, because a medication-free period may be required before starting a TCA to prevent serious side effects.
7. Report any worrisome or unusual changes in mood or behaviour to your physician.
8. This medication should be stored in a clean, dry area at room temperature to prevent the medication from breaking down.
9. Keep this and all medications out of the reach of children.

165.

Along with its beneficial effects, the medication may sometimes cause some unwanted effects. In most cases, these can be dealt with, and they may disappear as the medication is continued. Therefore, although side effects may be annoying, it is important you do not stop your medication without checking with your doctor first.

Side effects are usually not serious or troublesome. They will respond to appropriate treatment, and may decrease or disappear with time as your body adjusts to the medication.

There are two types of antidepressants.
Tricyclic antidepressants (TCA) are distributed under the trade names Amitriptyline, Amoxapine, Clomipramine, Desipramine, Doxepin, Imipramine, Protriptyline, and Trimipramine.

Mild side effects: Check with your doctor if any of the following side effects continue or are bothersome:

- Drowsiness and lethargy– This problem often goes away with time. If drowsiness does occur, avoid driving a car or operating machinery. Alcohol, sedatives, and antihistamines may worsen this effect. You might prevent these effects by taking the medications at bedtime. Talk to your physician or pharmacist.
- Dizziness– Get up from a lying or sitting position slowly. Dangle your legs over the edge of the bed for a few minutes before getting up. Sit or lie down if dizziness occurs.
- Nausea or heartburn– If these effects occur, take your medication with food.
- Dry mouth– Sucking sour candy or bits of ice, or chewing sugarless gum, may help to increase salivation. Drink water and brush your teeth regularly.
- Constipation– Increase bulk foods in the diet (e.g. bran, salads), exercise more often, drink plenty of fluids, and if necessary, use a bulk laxative (e.g., Metamucil).
- Blurred vision– Near vision may be affected, but this problem will usually disappear in about 1 week. Try reading under a bright light, from a distance, or wearing reading glasses.
- Sweating– You may sweat more than usual; talcum powder may be helpful.

166.

- Rapid heart rate-this effect is not usually dangerous, but let your doctor know.
- Muscle tremors or twitching.
- Changes in libido or sexual performance.
- Nightmares.

The TCA antidepressants are not habit-forming (i.e., addictive). However, if they are stopped suddenly after using them for a while, they may cause minor withdrawal symptoms such as muscle aches, chills, nausea, vomiting, and dizziness.

If you miss a dose of this medication (i.e., by more than 2-3 hours), skip the missed dose and continue with your next scheduled dose at the appropriate time. NEVER DOUBLE THE DOSE. If you miss more than one dose, contact your physician for further instructions.

Selective serotonin reuptake inhibitor (SSRI) antidepressants are distributed under the trade names Prozac, Luvox, Paxil and Zoloft.

Mild side effects: Check with your doctor if any of the following side effects continue or are bothersome:
- Stimulation, which occurs in some people taking this medication, may cause some nervousness, headache, agitation, trouble sleeping, or decreased appetite. This effect should be reported to the physician, and may be managed by taking the medication in the morning.
- Drowsiness and lethargy– This problem often goes away with time. If drowsiness does occur, avoid driving a car or operating machinery. Alcohol, sedatives, and antihistamines may worsen this effect.
- Dizziness– Get up from a lying or sitting position slowly. Dangle your legs over the edge of the bed for a few minutes before getting up. Sit or lie down if dizziness occurs.
- Nausea or heartburn– If these effects occur, take your medication with food.
- Dry mouth– Sucking sour candy or bits of ice, or chewing sugarless gum, may help to increase salivation. Drink water and brush your teeth regularly.

167.

- Constipation– Increase bulk foods in the diet (e.g., bran, salads), exercise more often, drink plenty of fluids, and if necessary, use a bulk laxative (e.g. Metamucil).
- Diarrhea
- Blurred vision– Near vision may be affected, but this problem will usually disappear in about 1 week. Try reading under a bright light, from a distance, or wearing reading glasses.
- Sweating– You may sweat more than usual; talcum powder may be helpful.
- Muscle tremors or twitching.
- Changes in libido or sexual performance.
- Nightmares.

If you miss a dose of this medication (i.e., by more than 5 hours), skip the missed dose and continue with your next scheduled dose at the appropriate time. NEVER DOUBLE THE DOSE. If you miss more than one dose, contact your physician for further instructions. The SSRI antidepressants are not considered to be habit-forming (i.e., addictive).

Side effects that should be reported immediately to your doctor include:
- soreness of the mouth, gums or throat
- skin rash or itching, swelling of the face
- fever or flu-like symptoms
- dark coloured urine
- difficulty urinating
- tingling in the hands and feet, severe muscle twitching
- persistent heartburn, severe nausea, vomiting
- switch in mood to an unusual state of happiness, irritability, or a marked disturbance in sleep.

Conditions which should be discussed with your doctor as soon as possible include:
- finding out you are pregnant
- deciding you are going to nurse your baby
- recurrence of depressive symptoms or fluctuation in mood

168.

If you have any questions, do not hesitate to contact either your doctor or your pharmacist.

Source: Addiction Research Foundation (1995).

BARBITURATES

Drug Class: Central Nervous System Depressants

Synopsis

Barbiturates are powerful depressants that slow down the central nervous system (CNS). Classified as sedative/hypnotics, they include amobarbital (e.g., Amytal), pen obarbital (e.g., Nembutal), phenobarbital (e.g., Luminal), secobarbital (e.g., Seconal), and the combination amobarbital-secobarbital (e.g., Tuinal). (Note that where a drug name is capitalized, it is a registered trade name of the manufacturer.)

What is discussed in this paper are most of the sedative/hypnotics that are not benzodiazepines. (For a discussion of benzodiazepines, see *Tranquillizers*.)

Barbiturates and other sedative/hypnotics are medically prescribed to treat sleeplessness, anxiety, and tension, and to help prevent or mitigate epileptic seizures. Certain barbiturates are also used to induce anesthesia for short surgical procedures or at the beginning of longer ones.

Because of the risks associated with barbiturate abuse, and because new and safer drugs such as benzodiazepines are now available, barbiturates are less frequently prescribed than in the past. Nonetheless, they are still available both on prescription and illegally.

Besides having therapeutic uses, barbiturates are often used for their pleasurably intoxicating effects. Some people take them in addition to alcohol, or as a substitute. Heavy users of other drugs sometimes turn to them if their usual drugs are not available, or to counteract the effects of large doses of stimulants such as amphetamines or cocaine.

Barbiturates are known generally on the street as "downers" or "barbs." Many are named for the colors of their brand-name versions – blues or blue heavens (Amytal), yellow jackets (Nembutal), red birds or red devils (Seconal) and rainbows or reds and blues (Tuinal).

169.

Effects

The effects of any drug depend on several factors:
- the amount taken at one time
- the user's past drug experience
- the manner in which the drug is taken
- the circumstances under which the drug is taken (the place, the user's psychological and emotional stability, the presence of other people, the simultaneous use of alcohol or other drugs, etc.).

Short-term effects are those that appear rapidly after a single dose and disappear within a few hours or days. With barbiturates, a small dose (e.g., 50 mg or less) may relieve anxiety and tension. A somewhat larger dose (e.g., 100 to 200 mg) will, in a tranquil setting, usually induce sleep. An equivalent dose in a social setting, however, may produce effects similar to those of drunkenness – a "high" feeling, slurred speech, staggering, slowed reactions, loss of inhibition, and intense emotions often expressed in an extreme and unpredictable manner. High doses characteristically produce slow, shallow, and irregular breathing, and can result in death from respiratory arrest.

Non-medical users often start taking barbiturates at doses within a safe therapeutic range. As tolerance develops, however, they progressively increase their daily dose to many times the original. It is extremely important to note that in spite of acquiring tolerance to the intoxicating effects of barbiturates, the user develops no tolerance to the lethal action of the drug. Therefore, high doses could produce fatal results even for tolerant abusers.

Taking barbiturates with other CNS depressants – e.g., alcohol; tranquillizers; such opioids as heroin, morphine, meperidine (Demerol), codeine, or methadone; and antihistamines (found in cold, cough, and allergy remedies) – can be extremely dangerous, even lethal.

No one should operate a motor vehicle or engage in tasks requiring concentration and coordination while under the influence of any CNS depressant.

The *long-term effect* of barbiturates - particularly of protracted high-dose abuse – is not unlike a state of chronic inebriation. Symptoms include the impairment of memory and judgment; hostility, depression, or mood swings; chronic fatigue; and stimulation of preexisting emotional disorders, which may result in paranoia or thoughts of suicide.

Although the prescribing of barbiturates has declined notably since the safer benzodiazepine tranquillizers were introduced, this group of drugs remains a significant contributor to drug-related deaths. They remain easily available to abusers through both licit and illicit sources.

Other Sedative/Hypnotics

Such drugs as glutethimide (Doriden), methyprylon (Noludar), ethchlorvynol (Placidyl), and methaqualone (found in Mandrax) were introduced as barbiturate substitutes, in the belief they would be safer. It was soon found, however, that they shared problems similar to those of barbiturates, including abuse leading to overdose and interaction with other CNS depressants. The same caution necessary in using barbiturates thus applies to these other sedative/hypnotics as well.

Tolerance and Dependence

Because *tolerance* to the intoxicating effects of sedative/hypnotics can develop rapidly with regular use, higher daily doses become necessary to achieve the desired effects. Taking more of the drug to compensate for tolerance, however, can lead to life-threatening complications. On one hand, there is the risk of death from overdose. On the other, when chronic and regular high-dose abuse has resulted in serious physical dependence, abrupt withdrawal can cause symptoms severe enough to cause death. For this reason, barbiturates are among the most dangerous of the widely abused drugs.

People who use these drugs daily for prolonged periods may become both psychologically and physically dependent upon them.

Psychological dependence exists when a drug is so central to a person's thoughts, emotions, and activities that the need to continue its use becomes a craving or compulsion. Psychological dependence is most likely to occur with the fast-acting barbiturates, which can produce euphoria within minutes of being taken.

Physical dependence exists when the body has adapted to the presence of the drug, and withdrawal symptoms occur when its use is abruptly ended. These symptoms range in intensity from progres-

171.

sive restlessness, anxiety, insomnia, and irritability to delirium and convulsions in severe cases. Again, it must be stressed that physical dependence on barbiturates can be one of the most dangerous of all drug dependencies.

Sedative/Hypnotics and Pregnancy

Studies link certain sedative/hypnotic drug use with birth defects and behavioral abnormalities in babies. Breathing difficulties have also been reported among infants, as have such withdrawal symptoms as irritability, disturbed sleep, and feeding difficulties.

Who Uses Barbiturates?

Barbiturates are commonly and heavily used by heroin addicts; they inject a mixture of both drugs to obtain a pleasurable "high" – a hazardous practice, because both drugs depress respiratory control centres in the brain. Some methamphetamine ("speed") abusers take barbiturates to combat severe hyperactivity following a "run" of methamphetamine use over several days.

A 1989 Addiction Research Foundation study of drug use in Ontario schools found that 7.8% of students in grades 7 to 13 reported having used prescribed barbiturates, and 2.9% nonprescribed barbiturates, at least once in the preceding year.

Barbiturates and the Law

Many barbiturates and other sedative/hypnotics are defined as controlled drugs, which are governed by Schedule G of Canada's *Food and Drugs Act*; the rest are governed by Schedule F. Drugs listed in Schedule F are legally available only with a physician's prescription. Additional restrictions apply to drugs listed in Schedule G.

It is illegal to obtain a prescription for any controlled drug without notifying a physician that you obtained a similar prescription through another practitioner within the preceding 30 days. Anyone convicted of trafficking in these drugs or possessing them for such a purpose is guilty of an offence that, if tried by indictment, carries a maximum penalty of 10 years imprisonment.

Source: Addiction Research Foundation (1991).

BENZODIAZEPINES

Drug Class: Anti-Anxiety Agents (Anxiolytics)/ Sedatives

Synopsis

Benzodiazepines are medications that are frequently prescribed for the symptomatic treatment of anxiety and sleep disorders. They produce their effects via specific receptors involving a neurochemical called gamma aminobutyric acid (GABA).

Because they are safer and more effective, benzodiazepines have replaced barbiturates in the treatment of both anxiety and insomnia. Benzodiazepines are also used as sedatives before some surgical and medical procedures, and for the treatment of seizure disorders and alcohol withdrawal.

The first benzodiazepine developed was chlordiazepoxide, which is sold under such trade names as Librium® and Apo-Chlordiazepoxide®. Diazepam (e.g., Valium®) was the next benzodiazepine to come on the market and, until the early 1980s, was the most widely prescribed benzodiazepine in the world. Now, newer benzodiazepines, such as lorazepam (e.g., Ativan®), alprazolam (e.g., Xanax®), and clonazepam (Rivotril®), account for most benzodiazepine prescriptions. (Where a name of a medication is capitalized, it is a registered trade name of the manufacturer.)

There are 16 different benzodiazepines currently available in Canada. Some are prescribed primarily for the treatment of anxiety (e.g., lorazepam, alprazolam and diazepam); others are recommended as sleeping medications (such as triazolam [e.g., Halcion®] and flurazepam [e.g., Dalmane®]). They remain the most commonly prescribed group of psychoactive (mood-altering) medications in Canada.

Even though they are effective, benzodiazepines do have some limitations and drawbacks. They may produce physical dependence, which results in a discontinuation or withdrawal syndrome when the medication is stopped. This syndrome is generally mild. However, stopping abruptly can produce a wide range of symptoms, including convulsions, especially if high doses have been used for a prolonged period of time. Benzodiazepines may also be misused and abused.

173.

Effects

The effects of any medication depend on several factors, including:
- the type and severity of the disorder for which the medication is prescribed
- the amount taken at one time
- the form in which the medication is taken
- the patient's age
- prior or concurrent use of psychoactive drugs
- the circumstances under which the medication is taken (i.e., the user's psychological and emotional state, simultaneous use of alcohol or other drugs, etc.).

A therapeutic dose of benzodiazepines (i.e., medically pre-scribed) can relieve anxiety and insomnia. Generally, benzodi-azepines are well tolerated and have a wide margin of safety. But some people may experience drowsiness, lethargy, dizziness or dif-ficulty with co-ordination.

High doses lead to heavier sedation and can impair both mental sharpness and physical co-ordination. Lower doses are recommend-ed for older people and for those with some chronic diseases, since they may be more sensitive to medications and may metabolize them more slowly. It has also been suggested that benzodiazepines can impair the ability to learn and remember new information.

Studies show that anti-anxiety agents, even when correctly pre-scribed, may interfere with the ability of some users to perform cer-tain physical, intellectual and perceptual functions. Most side-effects usually occur early in treatment and wane over time.

For these reasons, individuals should assess their response to benzodiazepines before they operate a motor vehicle or engage in tasks requiring concentration and co-ordination. Such activities may become more dangerous if benzodiazepines are used together with alcohol and/or other sedative/hypnotics or antihistamines (found in many cold, cough and allergy remedies).

Because some benzodiazepines (such as diazepam and flu-razepam) are metabolized and eliminated from the body quite slow-ly, the medication can accumulate in body tissues with long-term use and may heighten such effects as lethargy in some individuals. Some users may feel drowsy or "hung over," even on the day after they take the medication. Seniors, in particular, may be at increased risk of falls, fractures and confusion.

There have been very rare reports of unexpected stimulation resulting from benzodiazepine use, with cases ranging from agitation to violent behavior.

Toxic Effects

Overdoses of benzodiazepines, either accidental or intentional, do occur. While death rarely results from benzodiazepine overdose alone, these medications may be fatal when used in combination with alcohol and other drugs that depress the central nervous system.

Tolerance and Dependence

Tolerance is the need to increase the dose of a drug to maintain the desired effects. Tolerance to the anxiety-relieving effects of benzodiazepines is uncommon and most individuals do not increase their benzodiazepine dose. But tolerance to the sedative and other effects of benzodiazepines can develop in some people with regular use.

Risk of *physical dependence* increases if benzodiazepines are taken regularly (e.g., daily) for more than a few months, especially at higher than normal doses. However, problems have been reported after shorter periods of use. The user's body adapts to the presence of the medication and experiences withdrawal symptoms when use is stopped. The frequency and severity of these symptoms depend on the dosage, the duration of use, and whether the medication is stopped abruptly or tapered off.

Stopping abruptly can bring on such symptoms as trouble sleeping, gastrointestinal upset, feeling unwell, loss of appetite, sweating, trembling, weakness, anxiety, and changes in perception (e.g., numbness and altered sensitivity to light, sound and smells). In rare cases after high doses, psychosis and convulsions may occur.

The onset and severity of withdrawal are often more marked for benzodiazepines that are rapidly eliminated from the body (e.g., triazolam, alprazolam) than for those that are slowly eliminated (e.g., diazepam).

While most patients can tolerate such symptoms, a physician may decide to gradually taper the benzodiazepine dose to minimize discomfort, especially after long-term use. Gradual discontinuation

175.

of the medication is preferred, but it may not entirely eliminate withdrawal symptoms.

Diagnostic manuals recognize the occurrence of *psychological* or *behavioral dependence* on benzodiazepines. The main signs of psychological dependence on any drug are:

- a strong desire or craving for the drug
- seeking out the drug, often at the expense of other activities
- difficulty stopping or cutting down
- continued use despite physical or psychological consequences.

People who use benzodiazepines on a long-term basis to treat specific chronic disorders (such as panic disorder, social phobias or agoraphobia) rarely exhibit such symptoms or behaviors. On the other hand, psychological dependence has been clearly demonstrated among certain groups, such as polydrug abusers and methadone-treated heroin addicts.

Benzodiazepines and Pregnancy

A woman who is pregnant or thinking about becoming pregnant should know that benzodiazepines can affect her baby. Use of benzodiazepines during pregnancy may lead to withdrawal symptoms in the newborn. Also, they are passed on through breast milk and should be used with caution, if at all, while nursing. However, no one should stop taking the medication without consulting their physician first.

Who Uses Benzodiazepines?

In 1994, the Addiction Research Foundation (ARF) surveyed Ontario adults about their use of tranquillizers and sleeping pills. Benzodiazepines are included in both categories. Reported use of **tranquillizers** was 3.7% — a steady decline from 1977, when the reported level of use was 12.1%. This trend corresponds with other sources, including nationwide surveys. In Ontario, this decline has been significant among women, whose use fell to 4.1% in 1994 from 15.9% in 1977. In particular, women aged 50 and older have decreased their use (to 7.7% from 21%).

This survey also indicated that use of **sleeping pills** has increased from 6.5% in 1991 to 9.1% in 1994. However, rates of use between 1989 and 1994 do not vary significantly. Women are more likely than men to take sleeping pills, and their use increases with age. Of respondents who used tranquillizers and sleeping pills, 15.8% and 7.3% (respectively) were classified as dependent.

In a separate study done in 1993, ARF polled Ontario students from Grade 7 to OAC (formerly Grade 13). The findings showed that 2.2% reported using prescribed tranquillizers at least once in the preceding year; and 1.1% used non-prescribed tranquillizers. The self-reported rate of use was highest among 16- and 17-year-old students (3% for medical and 1.6% for non-medical purposes). These figures are less than half of those reported in 1987.

Certain segments of society may use benzodiazepines more frequently than others. For example, a 1990 ARF study found that many abused women report taking medications such as benzodiazepines to calm them or help them sleep. Individuals with alcohol, opioid or polydrug dependence may be at higher risk than others for benzodiazepine abuse and dependence. Staff at alcohol treatment and methadone maintenance programs report that some of their clients abuse or are dependent on benzodiazepines. Individuals dependent on other drugs should receive benzodiazepines only when the therapeutic indication is clear. Responses to therapy should be carefully monitored, as should dose and duration of treatment.

Benzodiazepines and the Law
Benzodiazepines are prescription drugs that are legally available to the public only through a physician's prescription.

Source: Addiction Research Foundation (1995).

CAFFEINE

Drug Class: Central Nervous System Stimulant

Synopsis
Caffeine is the world's most popular drug. The white, bitter-tasting, crystalline substance was first isolated from coffee in 1820. Both words, caffeine and coffee, are derived from the Arabic word qahweh (pronounced "kahveh" in Turkish). The origins of the words reflect the spread of the beverage into Europe via Arabia and

Turkey from north-east Africa, where coffee trees were cultivated in the 6th century. Coffee began to be popular in Europe in the 17th century. By the 18th century plantations had been established in Indonesia and the West Indies.

The caffeine content of coffee beans varies according to the species of the coffee plant. Beans from Coffea arabica, grown mostly in Central and South America, contain about 1.1% caffeine. Beans from Coffea robusta, grown mostly in Indonesia and Africa, contain about 2.2% caffeine. Caffeine also occurs in cacao pods and hence in cocoa and chocolate products; in kola nuts, used in the preparation of cola drinks; and in the ilex plant, from whose leaves the popular South American beverage yerba mate is prepared.

Caffeine is also found in tea. It was first isolated from tea leaves in 1827 and named "theine" because it was believed to be a distinctly different compound from the caffeine in coffee. Tea leaves contain about 3.5% caffeine, but a cup of tea usually contains less caffeine than a cup of coffee because much less tea than coffee is used during preparation.

In North America, the caffeine content of a cup of coffee averages about 75 mg, but varies widely according to cup size, the method of preparation, and the amount of coffee used. Generally, cups prepared from instant coffee contain less caffeine (average 65 mg) and cups prepared by drip methods contain more caffeine (average 110 mg). Cups of tea average about 30 mg, but the range is also large—from 10 to 90 mg.

Cola drinks contain about 35 mg caffeine per standard 280 mL serving, with some 5% of the caffeine being a component of kola nuts and most of the remainder being added in the form of a by-product of the decaffeination of coffee and tea. Caffeine-containing soft drinks account for more than 65% of soft drink consumption. A cup of hot chocolate contains about 4 mg caffeine, and a 50-gram chocolate bar between 5 and 60 mg, increasing with the quality of the chocolate. Caffeine is an ingredient of certain headache pills (30-65 mg). It is the main ingredient of non-prescription "stay-awake" pills (100-200 mg).

Short-Term Effects
Caffeine taken in beverage form begins to reach all tissues of the body within five minutes. Peak blood levels are reached in about 30

minutes. Half of a given dose of caffeine is metabolized in about four hours — more rapidly in smokers and less rapidly in newborn infants, in women in late pregnancy, and in sufferers from liver disease. Normally, almost all ingested caffeine is metabolized. Less than 3% appears unchanged in urine, and there is no day-to-day accumulation of the drug in the body.

Short-term effects of a drug are those that appear soon after a single dose and disappear within hours. Ingestion of the amount of caffeine in one or two cups of coffee (75-150 mg) causes many mild physiological effects. General metabolism increases — expressed as an increase in activity or raised temperature, or both. The rate of breathing increases, as does urination and the levels of fatty acids in the blood and of gastric acid in the stomach. (However, at least one other component of coffee also increases gastric acid secretion. Therefore ulcer sufferers may not achieve relief by switching to decaffeinated coffee.) Caffeine use may increase blood pressure.

Caffeine stimulates the brain and behavior. Use of 75-150 mg of caffeine elevates neural activity in many parts of the brain, postpones fatigue, and enhances performance at simple intellectual tasks and at physical work that involves endurance but not fine motor coordination. (Caffeine-caused tremor can reduce hand steadiness.)

Caffeine's effects on complex intellectual tasks and on mood do not lend themselves to a simple summary. The effects depend on the personality of the user, on the immediate environment, on the user's knowing whether caffeine has been taken, and even on the time of day.

The effects of caffeine on sleep are clear-cut: taken before bedtime, it usually delays sleep onset, shortens overall sleep time, and reduces the "depth" of sleep. After using caffeine, sleepers are more easily aroused, move more during sleep, and report a reduction in the quality of sleep. The effects of caffeine on dreaming are less clear.

Larger doses of caffeine, especially when given to non-users, can produce headache, jitteriness, abnormally rapid heartbeat (tachycardia), convulsions, and even delirium. Near-fatal doses cause a crisis resembling the state of a diabetic without insulin, including high levels of blood sugar and the appearance of acetone-like substances in urine. The lowest known dose fatal to an adult has been 3,200 mg — administered intravenously by accident. The fatal oral dose is in excess of 5,000 mg — the equivalent of 40 strong cups of coffee taken in a very short space of time.

Long-Term Effects

Long-term effects of a toxic nature do not appear evident when regular caffeine use is below about 650 mg a day — equivalent to about eight or nine average cups of coffee. Above this level, users may suffer from chronic insomnia, persistent anxiety and depression, and stomach ulcers. Caffeine use appears to be associated with irregular heartbeat and may raise cholesterol levels, but there is no firm evidence that caffeine causes heart disease.

The evidence is also unclear concerning caffeine and cancer. Caffeine and some of its metabolites can cause changes in the cells of the body and in the way in which they reproduce themselves, and caffeine certainly enhances this kind of action by some known carcinogens. However, although caffeine is suspected as a cause of cancer, the evidence is contradictory and does not allow a clear conclusion. Some animal studies suggest that caffeine can have anti-cancer properties. For example, in rats it prevents breast cancer caused by diethylstilbestrol (the "morning-after" pill).

Tolerance and Dependence

Tolerance refers to the body's "getting used" to a drug with its repeated taking. It is difficult to study the tolerance of human subjects to the various effects of caffeine because nearly everyone in our society uses caffeine regularly in one form or another. Careful research has suggested that tolerance develops to most of caffeine's effects — meaning that, with experience of the drug, the same dose produces a reduced effect, or a larger dose is required to produce the same level of effect.

Regular use of upwards of 350 mg of caffeine a day causes physical dependence on the drug. This means that interruption of the regular use produces a characteristic withdrawal syndrome, the most conspicuous feature of which is an often severe headache that can be relieved by taking caffeine. Absence of caffeine also makes regular users feel irritable and tired. Relief from these withdrawal effects is often given as a reason for using caffeine.

180.

Caffeine and Pregnancy

Caffeine certainly has the ability to cause a variety of reproductive effects in animals, including congenital abnormalities and reproductive failures, reduced fertility, prematurity, and low birth weight. What is unknown is whether these findings are relevant to the use of ordinary amounts of caffeine-containing beverages by pregnant women. Pregnant women have been advised to restrict caffeine intake by both Canadian and United States governments. Pregnant smokers should be especially wary.

Therapeutic Uses

The most common medicinal use of caffeine is as a part of headache preparations and other pain relievers. Caffeine is added both for its specific ability to relieve headache, including that caused by caffeine withdrawal, and for its ability to help analgesics do their work better.

The ability of caffeine to stimulate breathing is used in the treatment of apnea (cessation of breathing) in newborn babies, and as an antidote against the depression of breathing by overdoses of heroin and other opiate drugs.

More controversial therapeutic uses of caffeine are these: to kill skin funguses; to improve sperm mobility; to enhance the toxic effects of chemicals used in cancer therapy; and to facilitate the production of seizures during electroconvulsive therapy.

Who Uses Caffeine?

Annual world consumption of caffeine is about 120,000 tonnes — equivalent to 70 mg of the drug a day for each inhabitant. Of this total consumption, 54% is in the form of or derived from coffee; 43% is in the form of or derived from tea. Some three-quarters of the coffee that is cultivated is of the arabica species, but the robusta species accounts for rather more than a quarter of all caffeine derived from coffee because it contains twice as much caffeine.

Canadian consumption is close to 2,200 tonnes a year — 240 mg a day for each person. About 55% of this caffeine is consumed in the form of coffee, and about 32% in the form of tea. Soft drinks (with the caffeine coming mostly from decaffeinated coffee or tea) comprise another 7% of the Canadian total, and cocoa and chocolate products

181.

another 1%. The balance of 5% is accounted for by medicinal uses and beverages such as yerba mate.

In the United States, daily per-capita consumption of caffeine is about 210 mg. About 60% of United States consumption is in the form of coffee, with tea and soft drinks each accounting for about 16% of the total. Caffeine consumption is very much higher in some European countries. In Britain, daily per-capita use of caffeine is about 445 mg, about 72% of which is in the form of tea and 19% in the form of coffee. In Sweden, daily per-capita consumption is near 425 mg, 85% in the form of coffee and 6% in the form of tea.

Caffeine use has remained fairly consistent in Canada during the past three decades but has declined markedly in the United States, where coffee use per capita fell by 35% between 1960 and 1980. Soft drink consumption rose by 230% in the United States in the same period, but only by 65% in Canada.

The changes in the United States have occurred mainly among young people. Coffee has become a drink for older people.

There are wide ranges in caffeine use among individuals in both countries. Very roughly, 20% of adults in both Canada and the United States consume more than 350 mg caffeine each day and are therefore physically dependent on caffeine. Roughly 3% of adults in the United States and 4% in Canada consume more than 650 mg caffeine a day — enough to put their health in jeopardy.

* The figures in this section were gathered in the mid-1980s.
Source: Addiction Research Foundation (1991).

CANNABIS (MARIJUANA, HASHISH, HASHISH OIL)

Drug Class: Hallucinogen

Synopsis
Marijuana, hashish, and hashish oil are all products of the hemp plant Cannabis sativa, a hardy annual that grows in both tropical and temperate climates. The chief ingredient in the cannabis plant — the one that alters mood and perception — is called delta-9-tetrahydrocannabinol (THC).

182.

Although THC and other cannabis constituents have been tested for treatment of asthma, epilepsy, glaucoma, anorexia nervosa, and nausea caused by anti-cancer therapy, so far there are no generally accepted medical uses. Cannabis, however, is the most widely used illegal psychoactive drug in North America (with the possible exception of alcohol and tobacco used by minors).

Marijuana comes from the flowering tops and leaves of the dried plant, and frequently contains seeds and stems. It ranges in color from greyish-green to greenish-brown, and in texture from a fine substance resembling the herb oregano to a coarse substance that looks like tea. It is smoked in pipes or in hand-rolled cigarettes, called "joints."

Hashish, known as "hash," is the dried, caked resin from the flowers and leaves of the female plant. It usually contains a higher THC concentration than marijuana, and is therefore more potent. It is sold in either soft or hard chunks and ranges in color from light or medium brown to nearly black. Hash is usually mixed with tobacco and smoked in pipes or joints.

The most potent preparation other than pure THC is hash oil, a reddish-brown or green oily extract of cannabis, also called weed oil or honey oil on the street. Hash oil is usually dropped onto the end of a regular cigarette, or wiped onto the paper before it is rolled into a marijuana joint.

Pure THC, which can be produced synthetically in laboratories, is not available to street drug users because it is too difficult and expensive to make.

Cannabis is sometimes cooked in foods such as brownies, but in such cases the drug's effects are felt less rapidly, and are less under the control of the experienced user, than when it is smoked.

Effects
The effects of any drug depend on several factors:
- the amount taken at one time
- the user's past drug experience
- the manner in which the drug is taken
- the circumstances under which the drug is taken (the place, the user's emotions and activities, the presence of other people, the simultaneous use of alcohol or other drugs, etc.).

A very small amount of cannabis (e.g., containing 1 mg of THC) can produce a pleasurable "high" for the occasional user, and a single joint may be sufficient for two or three non-tolerant smokers. A heavy regular smoker may consume five or more joints a day. A marijuana joint the size of a cigarette typically contains between 2.5 and 5 mg of THC. More potent batches, however, are often sold on the street, so the dose may be higher than this.

Short-term effects appear soon after a single dose and disappear within a few hours or days. After a small amount of cannabis, the most common short-term effects are the "high" — a euphoric feeling marked by a tendency to talkativeness and laughter (similar, in many ways, to mild alcohol intoxication), a faster pulse rate, and reddened eyes. Later, the user becomes quiet, reflective, and sleepy.

With larger doses, these effects are enhanced, and the user may misjudge the passage of time; minutes may seem like hours. The user's sense of taste, touch, smell, sound, and color may also be sharpened or distorted.

Cannabis impairs concentration, short-term memory, logical thinking, and the ability to safely perform such complex tasks as operating a motor vehicle. Combined with alcohol, sedatives, and various other drugs, cannabis heightens their effects on thinking, behavior, and muscle control.

With extreme doses, the effects of cannabis are similar to those of LSD and other hallucinogens. (See *LSD* and *Hallucinogens.*) Some users experience an acute toxic psychosis, characterized by hallucinations, paranoid delusions, disorientation, and intense feelings of depersonalization (the belief that one is "unreal"). These symptoms are usually temporary, but cannabis can also unmask latent schizophrenia, which may continue indefinitely.

Long-term effects of cannabis — those following repeated use over a lengthy period — have only quite recently become the subject of extensive research. Most findings are preliminary, and sometimes contradictory. There is good evidence, however, that long-term heavy cannabis smoking is particularly harmful to the respiratory system. The tar content of cannabis smoke is much higher than that of tobacco.

Chronic heavy users, especially teens and young adults, sometimes display a lack of energy and ambition, loss of memory, and poor judgment. This has been called the "amotivational syndrome"

— but because those affected are usually multiple-drug users, it is difficult to know what specific role cannabis plays in such cases.

Some physicians treating marijuana users have associated the following disturbances with long, consistent use: chromosome damage, low levels of male sex hormone, reduced defences against infection, and brain damage. Although these effects have not been proven to be linked directly with marijuana use in humans, animal experiments show that high doses of cannabis can cause them.

Tolerance and Dependence

After taking cannabis for a few consecutive days, users develop a sensitivity to the drug; they experience the mood-altering effects more quickly, even with a smaller amount than was taken at first. With frequent and long use, however, they develop tolerance, which makes larger amounts necessary to produce the initial effects

With regular use, people can become psychologically dependent on cannabis. They develop a persistent craving for its mood-altering effects and feel uncomfortable and anxious if the drug is temporarily unavailable.

Physical dependence may develop in those who use high doses of cannabis on a daily basis. Quitting abruptly can produce a mild withdrawal syndrome, with such symptoms as troubled sleep, irritability, anxiety, sweating, and loss of appetite. Such withdrawal symptoms usually last less than a week.

Cannabis and Pregnancy

Cannabis use during pregnancy can retard fetal growth and result in mild withdrawal symptoms in the newborn. Experiments with animals also suggest that prenatal exposure retards the baby's growth and behavior.

Who Uses Cannabis?

In a 1989 survey of Ontario high school students, about one in seven admitted smoking marijuana at least once in the preceding year; only a small number reported daily smoking. In an adult survey the same year, 10.5% — most of them under 30 and more males than females — said they had used the drug in the previous 12 months.

185.

A key factor in the higher rate of occasional cannabis use among students compared to adults may be that the majority of young users are experimenters: they try cannabis on only a few occasions, then stop using it. It is possible that after satisfying their curiosity they lose interest, or, after bowing to peer pressure to try it, they feel no more pressure to use it.

Cannabis and the Law

Cannabis is governed by Canada's *Narcotic Control Act*. If tried by summary conviction, a first offence for possession carries a maximum penalty of a $1,000 fine and six months imprisonment. For subsequent offences, the maximum penalty is a $2,000 fine and 12 months imprisonment.

If tried by indictment, cannabis possession carries a maximum penalty of seven years imprisonment.

Importing, exporting, trafficking, and possession for the purposes of trafficking are all indictable offences and carry a maximum penalty of life imprisonment.

Cultivation of cannabis is also an indictable offence and carries a maximum penalty of seven years imprisonment.

Source: Addiction Research Foundation (1991).

COCAINE

Drug Class: Central Nervous System Stimulant

Synopsis

Cocaine is a powerful central nervous system (CNS) stimulant that heightens alertness, inhibits appetite and the need for sleep, and provides intense feelings of pleasure. It is prepared from the leaf of the Erythroxylon coca bush, which grows primarily in Peru and Bolivia.

Pure cocaine was first extracted and identified by the German chemist Albert Niemann in the mid-19th century, and was introduced as a tonic/elixir in patent medicines to treat a wide variety of real or imagined illnesses. Later, it was used as a local anesthetic for eye, ear, and throat surgery and continues today to have limited employment in surgery. Currently, it has no other clinical application, having been largely replaced by synthetic local anesthetics such as lidocaine.

Because of its potent euphoric and energizing effects, many people in the late 19th century took cocaine, even though some physicians recognized that users quickly became dependent. In the 1880s, the psychiatrist Sigmund Freud created a sensation with a series of papers praising cocaine's potential to cure depression, alcoholism, and morphine addiction.

Skepticism soon replaced this excitement, however, when documented reports of fatal cocaine poisoning, alarming mental disturbances, and cocaine addiction began to circulate.

According to information collected in 1902, 92% of all cocaine sold in major cities in the United States was in the form of an ingredient in tonics and potions available from local pharmacies.

In 1911, the Canadian government legally restricted cocaine use, and its popularity waned. The 1920s and '30s saw a marked decline in its use, especially after amphetamines became easily available. Cocaine's return to popularity, beginning in the late 1960s, coincided with the decreased use of amphetamines.

Appearance

Cocaine is generally sold on the street as a hydrochloride salt —a fine, white crystalline powder known as coke, C, snow, flake, or blow. Street dealers dilute it with inert (non-psychoactive) but similar-looking substances such as cornstarch, talcum powder, and sugar, or with active drugs such as procaine and benzocaine (used as local anesthetics), or other CNS stimulants such as amphetamines. Nevertheless, illicit cocaine has actually become purer over the years; according to RCMP figures, in 1988 its purity averaged about 75%.

Cocaine in powder form is usually "snorted" into the nostrils, although it may also be rubbed onto the mucous lining of the mouth, rectum, or vagina. To experience cocaine's effects more quickly, and to heighten their intensity, users sometimes inject it.

Cocaine hydrochloride can be chemically altered to remove other substances. The process, called "freebasing," is potentially dangerous because the solvents used are highly flammable. The pure form of cocaine that results ("free base") is smoked rather than

187.

snorted. The drug commonly called "crack" is a crude form of free base that has become popular in recent years.

Effects

The effects of any drug depend on several factors:
- the amount taken at one time
- the user's past drug experience
- the manner in which the drug is taken
- the circumstances under which the drug is taken (the place, the user's psychological and emotional stability the presence of other people, the simultaneous use of alcohol or other drugs, etc.).

Cocaine's short-term effects appear soon after a single dose and disappear within a few minutes or hours. Taken in small amounts (up to 100 mg), cocaine usually makes the user feel euphoric, energetic, talkative, and mentally alert — especially to the sensations of sight, sound, and touch. It can also temporarily dispel the need for food and sleep. Paradoxically, it can make some people feel contemplative, anxious, or even panic-stricken. Some people find that the drug helps them perform simple physical and intellectual tasks more quickly; others experience just the opposite effect.

Physical symptoms include accelerated heartbeat and breathing, and higher blood pressure and body temperature.

Large amounts (several hundred milligrams or more) intensify users' "high," but may also lead to bizarre, erratic, and violent behavior. These users may experience tremors, vertigo, muscle twitches, paranoia, or, with repeated doses, a toxic reaction closely resembling amphetamine poisoning.

Physical symptoms may include chest pain, nausea, blurred vision, fever, muscle spasms, convulsions, and coma. Death from a cocaine overdose can occur from convulsions, heart failure, or the depression of vital brain centres controlling respiration.

With repeated administration over time, users experience the drug's long-term effects. Euphoria is gradually displaced by restlessness, extreme excitability, insomnia, and paranoia — and eventually hallucinations and delusions. These conditions, clinically identical to amphetamine psychosis and very similar to paranoid schizophrenia, disappear rapidly in most cases after cocaine use is ended.

188.

While many of the physical effects of heavy continuous use are essentially the same as those of short-term use, the heavy user may also suffer from mood swings, paranoia, loss of interest in sex, weight loss, and insomnia.

Chronic cocaine snorting often causes stuffiness, runny nose, eczema around the nostrils, and a perforated nasal septum. Users who inject the drug risk not only overdosing but also infections from unsterile needles and hepatitis or AIDS (acquired immune deficiency syndrome) from needles shared with others. Severe respiratory tract irritation has been noted in some heavy users of cocaine free base.

Tolerance and Dependence

Tolerance to any drug exists when higher doses are necessary to achieve the same effects once reached with lower doses. But scientists have not observed tolerance to cocaine's stimulant effect: users may keep taking the original amount over extended periods and still experience the same euphoria. Yet some users frequently increase their dose to intensify and prolong the effects. Amounts up to 10 g (10,000 mg) have been reported.

Some users, however, report that they become more sensitive to cocaine's anesthetic and convulsant effects even without increasing the amount. This theory of increased sensitivity has been put forward to explain some deaths that have occurred after apparently low doses.

Psychological dependence exists when a drug is so central to a person's thoughts, emotions, and activities that it becomes a craving or compulsion. Among heavy cocaine users, an intense psychological dependence can occur; they suffer severe depression if the drug is unavailable, which lifts only when they take it again.

Experiments with animals suggest that cocaine is perhaps the most powerful drug of all in producing psychological dependence. Rats and monkeys made dependent on cocaine will always strive hard to get more.

At present, researchers do not agree on what constitutes physical dependence on cocaine. When regular heavy users stop taking the drug, however, they experience what they term the "crash" shortly afterwards.

Overall, during abstinence, many users complain of sleep and eating disorders, depression, and anxiety, and the craving for cocaine

189.

often compels them to take it again. Treatment of the dependent cocaine user is therefore difficult, and the relapse rate is high. Nevertheless, some heavy users have been able to quit on their own.

Cocaine and Pregnancy

There is little research on cocaine's effects on pregnant women or the fetus. One preliminary report suggests that its tendency to raise blood pressure may increase the risk of obstetrical complications. Studies of the effects of crack use on offspring have been reported, but the possible contribution to these effects of other factors, including use of other drugs — such as alcohol, cannabis, and tobacco — is difficult to assess.

Who Uses Cocaine?

The initial resurgence of cocaine use in the 1960s was largely confined to the affluent, for it was at that time quite expensive. Part of the drug's mystique was its association with celebrities in the music, sports and show business worlds. Today, people from all walks of life use cocaine. Young single people are the most frequent users, with male users outnumbering female users two to one.

There are no clear connections between cocaine use and education, occupation, or socioeconomic status.

Most people who use cocaine use it only occasionally. Even though cocaine costs less today and is generally of higher quality than in the past, fewer than 10% of those who ever try the drug use it once a week or more.

Surveys of Canadian adults and high school students showed that throughout the 1980s use of the drug remained stable — and even declined at times. A 1989 Addiction Research Foundation survey of Ontario students in grades 7 to 13 found that 2.7% reported using cocaine at least once in the preceding year.

Cocaine and the Law

Cocaine falls under Canada's *Narcotic Control Act*. (Pharmacologically, the term "narcotic" is applied only to the opiate drugs; however, this Act deals with other illicit drugs such as cocaine and cannabis.)

If tried by summary conviction, a first offence for cocaine possession carries a maximum penalty of a $1,000 fine and six months imprisonment. For subsequent offences, the maximum penalty is a

$2,000 fine and 12 months imprisonment. If tried by indictment, cocaine possession carries a maximum penalty of seven years imprisonment. Trafficking, importing, exporting, and possession for the purposes of trafficking are all indictable offences and carry a maximum penalty of life imprisonment.

Source: Addiction Research Foundation (1991).

HALLUCINOGENS

Synopsis

The term "hallucinogen" describes any drug that radically changes a person's mental state by distorting the perception of reality to the point where, at high doses, hallucinations occur. These drugs have also been labelled illusionogenic, psychotomimetic, psychedelic, and mind-expanding depending on whether scientists or users are talking about them.

Hallucinogens include a wide variety of substances, which are different from each other in structure and range from wholly synthetic products to natural plant extracts. Mescaline can be manufactured synthetically or extracted from the peyote cactus. Similarly, psilocybin can be chemically produced or extracted from certain mushrooms.

Other hallucinogens are found in such naturally occurring materials as morning glory seeds, jimson weed, nutmeg, and a variety of mushrooms. Cannabis, often classified as a hallucinogen, is also from a plant source (see *Facts About Cannabis*).

Such drugs as DMT, LSD, MDA, PCP, PMA, STP (DOM), and TMA are synthetic chemicals manufactured in illegal "underground" laboratories specifically for the illicit drug market.

Such other drugs as amphetamines and alcohol, although not usually classified as hallucinogens, and cannabis can surprise the user by producing hallucinations and related effects when taken in very large doses and in certain circumstances.

Effects

The effects of any drug depend on several factors:
- the amount taken at one time
- the user's past drug experience

- the manner in which the drug is taken
- the circumstances under which the drug is taken (the place, the user's emotions and activities, the presence of other people, simultaneous use of alcohol or other drugs, etc.).

The effects of any hallucinogen and the users's reaction to it can differ significantly among individuals, and can range from ecstasy to terror. In fact, during any one hallucinogenic episode, a user is likely to experience various psychic and emotional reactions.

In low doses, the hallucinogens produce a spectrum of effects depending on the properties of the particular drug and the individual user's sensitivity. These effects include alterations in mood and perception. More severe effects, such as hallucinations, are most likely to occur at high doses.

Users may experience different reactions to the same drug on different occasions, finding the effects at times pleasant and at other times disturbing and threatening. Although the differences may be due in part to the wide variations in the composition and quality of illicit drugs, it also happens when the drugs are known to be pure and the doses on different occasions are equal.

Tolerance and Dependence

Regular use of such hallucinogens as LSD, mescaline, and psilocybin induce tolerance within a few days: that is, little or no effect is experienced even with high doses. *Cross-tolerance* develops among LSD, mescaline, psilocybin, and DMT; that is, a person who has built up tolerance to one of these drugs will be unable to experience the effects of any of the other three. Normal sensitivity is usually restored after abstaining for several consecutive days.

Chronic users may also become psychologically dependent on hallucinogens. Psychological dependence exists when a drug is so central to a person's thoughts, emotions, and activities that the need to continue its use amounts to a craving or compulsion.

Hallucinogens do not appear to cause physical dependence, for withdrawal reactions have not been observed, even after long-term use.

Hallucinogens and Pregnancy

LSD use by pregnant women appears to be associated with an increased risk of spontaneous abortion. Research also suggests that it may be linked to a higher incidence of congenital abnormalities among users' babies. Early studies associating the use of LSD with chromosome damage have not been confirmed conclusively.

Little is known about the effects of other hallucinogens on the pregnant woman and her fetus.

Hallucinogens and the Law

Psilocybin, DMT, LSD, MDA, PMA, and STP (DOM) are classified as restricted drugs in Schedule H of Canada's *Food and Drugs Act*. It is thus illegal to possess these drugs without government authorization, which is given only to qualified laboratory and research personnel conducting approved clinical and experimental investigations.

If tried by summary conviction, possession (first offence) carries a maximum penalty of a $1,000 fine and six months imprisonment. For a subsequent offence, the maximum penalty is a $2,000 fine and one year imprisonment. If tried by indictment, a conviction for possession carries a maximum penalty of a $5,000 fine and three years imprisonment.

Trafficking and possession for that purpose, if tried by summary conviction, carry a maximum penalty of 18 months, and, if tried by indictment, 10 years imprisonment.

Possession, selling, importing, and exporting of PCP are prohibited under the *Narcotic Control Act*. If tried by summary conviction, possession carries a maximum penalty of $1,000 and six months imprisonment for a first offence, and $2,000 and one year imprisonment for a subsequent conviction. If tried by indictment, however, possession may result in imprisonment for up to seven years. Importing, exporting, trafficking, and possession for the purpose of trafficking are indictable offences and carry a maximum penalty of life imprisonment.

Of all the hallucinogens mentioned, only mescaline can be legally sold on prescription, although it rarely is.

Morning glory seeds, peyote, nutmeg, and jimson weed are not subject to any legal restrictions in Canada.

Individual Drug Prescriptions

What follows is a drug-by-drug description of the various hallucinogens and their respective effects. The drugs are grouped according to similarities in structure and/or source.

LSD, Psilocybin, DMT, Morning Glory Seeds

LSD

Commonly called "acid," LSD (lysergic acid diethylamide) is a semisynthetic alkaloid derived from lysergic acid, a substance found in ergot, a fungus growing on rye and other grains.

Pure LSD is a white, odorless crystalline powder. For street sales, it is generally mixed with colored substances and sold in capsules, tablets, or liquid form. For easier handling, LSD is also often spotted onto gelatin sheets or blotting paper. It is usually taken orally, but may be "snorted" into the nose or injected. Because of its high potency, very small amounts are effective. Street doses are highly variable, often ranging in strength from 40 to 700 micrograms per "hit" (1,000 micrograms equals 1 milligram).

The initial effects of this drug are generally felt in less than an hour, last from two to 12 hours, and then gradually taper off. Physical effects include increased blood pressure, dilated pupils, and rapid heartbeat. Muscular weakness, trembling, nausea, chills, and hyperventilation (breathing too deeply and rapidly) occur frequently. Motor skills and coordination may be impaired.

The drug, however, is used primarily for its striking effects on perception, thought, and mood. The user may experience several different emotions at the same time or swing rapidly from one mood to another. Hearing, smell, and vision may be intensified or merged, and sense of time and space may also be affected.

LSD diminishes the user's capacity to distinguish the boundaries between one object and another, and to differentiate the self from the environment. For some, this is a pleasant sensation, but for others it may induce panic. Some LSD users have experienced prolonged serious depression, anxiety, and even psychotic reactions.

Another possible after-effect of LSD use is the "flashback," a spontaneous recurrence of the sensations that occurred during a previous drug experience. A flashback can occur days, weeks, or even years after LSD use. The effects may range from pleasant to severely disturbing.

Although there are no known deaths directly attributable to the pharmacological effects of LSD in humans, there have been reports of deaths due to LSD-associated accidents and suicides.

Psilocybin

Psilocybin is the active ingredient in the Psilocybe mexicana mushroom and some other mushroom species. Psilocin is an accompanying alkaloid, usually present in small amounts. Psilocybin and psilocin are derivatives of tryptamine, and are chemically related to both LSD and DMT.

Pure psilocybin is a white crystalline substance, but the drug also may be distributed in crude mushroom preparations, in dried brown mushrooms, or as a capsule containing a powdered material of any color. It is usually taken orally, but may also be injected. Doses of the pure compound generally vary from 4 to 10 mg, although amounts up to 60 mg are not unusual.

The initial effects of this drug are felt after approximately half an hour and usually last several hours. A small dose (4 to 8 mg) may produce sensations of mental and physical relaxation, fatigue, detachment from surroundings, and sometimes feelings of physical heaviness or, conversely, lightness. Changes in mood and vivid perceptual distortion (particularly visual) may also occur. Thought patterns are disrupted, and intense preoccupation with trivial details often occurs. Users often report profound mystical or religious experiences.

Larger doses (13 mg or more) can produce dizziness; lightheadedness; abdominal discomfort; numbness of tongue, lips, or mouth; nausea; anxiety; and shivering. Marked changes in perception gradually develop, and the user experiences effects similar to those of LSD. Other reported effects include a sense of time passing slowly, yawning, facial flushing, sweating, depersonalization (a feeling of separation from one's body), feelings of unreality, and inability to concentrate.

The substance purchased on the street as psilocybin is only occasionally the pure drug. More often such drugs as LSD and PCP are misrepresented as psilocybin.

DMT

DMT (dimethyltryptamine) is a synthetic chemical resembling psilocin, an alkaloid contained in the Psilocybe mexicana mushroom. It is also present in some other plant substances, such as Piptadina peregrina.

DMT is usually consumed along with marijuana, which is soaked in a solution of DMT and then dried and smoked in a pipe or cigarette. It can also be made into a tea.

The effects, which are similar to those of LSD, begin almost immediately after ingestion and last approximately 30 to 60 minutes. Anxiety reactions and panic states are more frequently associated with DMT than with other hallucinogens, probably because of the unexpected rapidity of its effects.

Morning Glory Seeds

Lysergic acid amide, the predominant active ingredient in morning glory seeds, is chemically related to LSD, but is approximately one-tenth as potent.

The seeds themselves are brown or black, and may be eaten whole or ground. If eaten whole, they will likely pass through the digestive tract with little effect on the user. When seeds are chewed, effects begin within approximately 30 to 90 minutes and are similar to those of LSD. Depending on the variety of the seeds, an estimated 300 would produce effects equivalent to those of a 200 to 300 microgram dose of LSD.

Lysergic acid amide may also be extracted from the seeds and injected to produce a more immediate and intense experience.

Morning glory seeds are packaged commercially and sold legally. Many varieties have been treated with insecticides, fungicides, or other chemicals that can prove poisonous if enough seeds are consumed. Some varieties have also been specially treated to induce nausea if eaten.

Mescaline, MDA, PMA, STP (DOM) TMA, Nutmeg, PCP, Jimson Weed

Mescaline

Mescaline is prepared from the peyote cactus. The heads or "buttons" of the cactus are dried and then sliced, chopped, or ground,

---

---

and sometimes put in capsules. Mescaline may also be synthesized as a powder and distributed in capsule or tablet form, although the synthetic product is almost never available to illicit users.

Mescaline is usually taken orally, but can be inhaled by smoking ground peyote "buttons" or (more rarely) injected. It is considerably less potent than LSD, with an average dose ranging from 300 to 500 mg. In Canada, of the alleged mescaline samples submitted for drug analysis, hardly any are true mescaline. They usually contain PCP, or PCP combined with LSD.

At low doses, effects appear slowly and last from 1 to 18 hours. Physical effects include dilated pupils, higher body temperature, some muscular relaxation, nausea, and vomiting. The common mental effects include euphoria, heightened sensory perception, visual hallucinations (characteristically including brightly colored zigzag lines or geometric patterns - which the user knows are imaginary), perceived alterations of one's body image, and difficulty in thinking. Reports of mystical or religious experiences are common.

High doses can cause headache, dry skin, hypotension (low blood pressure), cardiac depression, and a slowing of the respiratory rate.

MDA

MDA (methylenedioxyamphetamine) is chemically related both to mescaline and to the amphetamines (see *Amphetamines*). It is prepared as a white to light brown powder and occasionally as an amber liquid. MDA is usually swallowed, but it may be sniffed or injected. The common dose is 120 mg and upward. Other drugs such as PCP are frequently misrepresented to be MDA.

At low doses, effects appear 30 to 60 minutes after ingestion and persist for approximately eight hours. Users generally report a sense of well-being along with heightened tactile sensations, intensification of feelings, and increased self-insight. Higher doses produce effects similar to those of LSD, including hallucinations or sensory distortions. Physical effects resemble those of amphetamines, and include dilated pupils, high blood pressure, and dry nose and throat. These effects are not usually very pronounced at low doses.

Occasionally, adverse after-effects do occur, usually in the form of marked physical exhaustion coupled with anxiety, lasting up to two days. At high doses, serious physical reactions requiring immediate medical treatment have occurred, and MDA-associated deaths and near deaths have been reported.

Less Frequently-Encountered Substances
PMA
PMA (paramethoxyamphetamine) is a rarely encountered and highly toxic drug that has both hallucinogenic and central nervous system (CNS) stimulant properties. Although the pure drug is a white powder, it appeared on the street in Ontario in a variety of forms in the mid-1970s and was responsible for several deaths. On the street, PMA has been passed off as MDA. Yet at a dose considered safe for MDA, PMA is highly toxic because it produces marked increases in blood pressure, body temperature, and pulse rate.

Because it is more potent, PMA also has more pronounced hallucinogenic and stimulant effects than MDA. The physical effects generally include greatly increased pulse rate and blood pressure, increased and labored respiration, escalating body temperature, erratic eye movements, muscle spasm, nausea, and vomiting. At high doses, PMA use can result in convulsions, coma, and death.

STP (DOM)
Another drug rarely encountered in recent years is STP, also known as DOM (4-methyl-2,5-dimethoxyamphetamine), a substance chemically related to mescaline and the amphetamines. Usually taken orally, this drug is considerably more potent than mescaline, but less potent than LSD.

Physical effects can include sleeplessness, dry mouth, nausea, blurred vision, sweating, flushed skin, and shaking. Exhaustion, confusion, excitement, delirium, and convulsions may also occur. Severe adverse reactions ("bad trips") are frequent, and the effects may last from 16 to 24 hours. Although there are no reports of deaths directly attributable to STP, users who have already experienced psychological disturbances may suffer a prolonged psychotic reaction.

TMA
TMA (trimethoxyamphetamine) is equally uncommon on the street, although drug dealers sometimes pass off MDA or other hal-

198.

lucinogens as TMA. A hallucinogen with stimulant properties, which generally appears as a yellow or beige powder, TMA is more potent than mescaline. It may be taken orally or injected. After approximately two hours, the user experiences intensified auditory and tactile sensations and mescaline-like hallucinations. There has been insufficient research to permit conclusions about after-effects, adverse reactions, overdose, or addiction potential.

Nutmeg

The known active ingredient in nutmeg (Myristica fragrans) is elemicin, a compound chemically related to mescaline and TMA. Nutmeg powder is eaten or sometimes "snorted."

Low doses may produce mild and brief euphoria, lightheaded-ness, and CNS stimulation. At higher doses, there may be rapid heartbeat, excessive thirst, agitation, anxiety, acute panic, vomiting, and hallucinations. The effects begin slowly and last several hours; they may be followed by drowsiness.

Although nutmeg is readily available, it apparently is general-ly used only when other hallucinogens are not obtainable. Recovery from nutmeg intoxication is slow and often involves unpleasant hangover effects.

PCP

PCP (phencyclidine) has both general anesthetic and hallucinogenic properties. It often appears as white or colored chunks or crystals. It is also found as a powder and in tablet or capsule form. PCP is usu-ally mixed with tobacco, marijuana, or dried parsley and smoked, but may also be "snorted," taken orally or injected. The usual dose is from 2 to 10 mg. The strength of the dose in street samples, howev-er, is more highly unpredictable than with most street drugs.

In low doses, PCP produces muscle stiffness and incoordina-tion, slurred speech, drowsiness, confusion, and general numbness of the extremities. Euphoria is experienced by many users. Nausea and vomiting may also develop, as well as profuse sweating, flush-ing, and increased heart rate.

At high doses, anesthesia may occur. Perceptual distortions and feelings of apathy, estrangement, or isolation may also be experi-enced. Strange and violent behavior can occur. In some cases, effects

199.

have lasted from 10 days to two weeks. Death may result from severe side effects induced by large doses (uncontrollable convulsions, respiratory depression, high fever, and a sudden surge of blood pressure resulting in intracranial hemorrhage), or from injuries related to the behavioral effects of the drug. Flashbacks and periods of prolonged anxiety, severe depression, or psychotic symptoms can occur with heavy users.

Jimson Weed

In high doses, the belladonna alkaloids present in jimson weed (Datura stramortium) can produce hallucinations. These hallucinogenic alkaloids are present in various proportions in all parts of the plant, but usually the leaves or berries are eaten. They produce marked dryness of the mouth, dilated pupils, hot dry skin, blurred vision, raised body temperature, rapid heartbeat, constipation, and difficulty urinating.

Source: Addiction Research Foundation (1991).

INHALANTS

Drug Class: Sedative/Hypnotics, Anesthetics

Synopsis

Almost all commonly abused inhalants are volatile hydrocarbon solvents produced from petroleum and natural gas; the two main exceptions are amyl nitrite and nitrous oxide. ("Volatile" means the hydrocarbons evaporate when exposed to air, and "solvents" refers to their capacity, in liquid form, to dissolve many other substances.)

Volatile hydrocarbon solvents have an enormous number of industrial, commercial, and household uses. They are found, for example, in cleaning fluid (e.g., benzene, trichloroethane), gasoline (benzene, toluene, xylene), nail polish remover (e.g., acetone), lighter fluid (e.g., naphtha), model airplane glue and lacquer thinners (e.g., toluene, xylene), and plastic cement (e.g., hexane). Other common ones are used in some felt-tipped pens and typewriter correction fluids.

200.

Certain hydrocarbons provide the pressurized propellant in such aerosol products as cookware coating agents, deodorants, hair sprays, insecticides, paints, and some medications. They are also used as anesthetics.

Abuse of volatile hydrocarbons — inhalants — is not new. Getting "high" by inhaling ether or nitrous oxide was common in Europe, Great Britain, and North America during the 1800s. In the 1960s widespread sniffing of the solvents in model airplane glue and nail polish remover began.

When aerosols were first brought on the market, they contained fluorocarbons, which, when sniffed, resulted in many fatal accidents. Because of growing abuse and also environmental concerns about the earth's ozone layer, fluorocarbons in aerosols have been replaced with hydrocarbons. It is unknown as yet how effective this measure will be.

Effects

The effects of any drug depend on several factors:
- the amount taken at one time
- the user's past drug experience
- the manner in which the drug is taken
- the circumstances under which the drug is taken (the place, the user's emotions and activities, the presence of other people, the simultaneous use of alcohol or other drugs, etc.).

Inhaled vapors from solvents and propellants enter the bloodstream directly from the lungs and are then rapidly distributed to the brain and liver — those organs with the largest blood supply. Most volatile hydrocarbons are fat-soluble, and are thus absorbed quickly into the central nervous system. Their action slows down breathing and heart rate.

While some volatile hydrocarbons are metabolized and then excreted through the kidneys, many are eliminated from the body unchanged, primarily through the lungs. The odor of solvents may therefore remain on the breath for several hours following inhalation. The complete elimination of volatile hydrocarbons may take some time, since they are released slowly from fatty tissues back into the blood.

Short-term effects appear soon after inhalation and disappear within a few hours. After inhaling there is a euphoric feeling, characterized by lightheadedness, exhilaration, and vivid fantasies. Nausea, drooling, sneezing and coughing, muscular incoordination, slow reflexes, and sensitivity to light may also occur. Some users' feelings of being very powerful may lead to reckless and bizarre behavior. Solvent abuse has been linked with such antisocial activities as dangerous driving, property damage, and theft.

Deep, repeated inhalation over short periods may result in a loss of control, culminating in hallucinations, unconsciousness, or seizures.

The effects of the first brief inhalation fade after several minutes. The experienced user, however, may prolong the effects for up to 12 hours, increasing the dose by concentrating the drug inside a plastic bag and continuing to sniff. For the majority of users, most effects disappear within an hour after sniffing is stopped, although hangovers and headaches may last several days.

A number of deaths have been associated with acute inhalant abuse, most prominently "sudden sniffing deaths" and suffocations. Sudden sniffing death, which typically follows strenuous exercise or undue stress after several deep inhalations, is caused by heart failure resulting from severely irregular heartbeat. Death by suffocation has occurred after users have fallen asleep or become unconscious with a plastic bag over nose and mouth. Some accidental deaths have been due to bizarre behavior caused by sniffing.

Long-term effects appear following repeated use over a lengthy period and include such physical effects as pallor, thirst, weight loss, nosebleeds, bloodshot eyes, and sores on the nose and mouth. Some solvents, such as aromatic hydrocarbons (e.g., benzene), interfere with formation of blood cells in bone marrow, while others may impair liver and kidney function. Although these effects generally disappear when use is stopped, some cleaning fluids (trichloroethane) and aerosol propellants (fluorocarbons) can cause permanent liver and kidney damage. Alcohol use may compound the damage.

Behavioral symptoms in regular heavy sniffers include mental confusion, fatigue, depression, irritability, hostility, and paranoia. Signs of brain damage, including severely impaired mental function, lack of motor coordination, and tremors, have been noted in

202.

heavy users of toluene (found in contact cement). Gasoline sniffing may produce behavioral changes due to lead poisoning.

Tolerance and Dependence

Regular inhalant use induces tolerance, which means increased doses are necessary to produce the same effects. After a year, for example, a regular glue sniffer may be using from eight to ten tubes of plastic cement to maintain the "high" originally achieved with a single tube.

Psychological dependence on solvents — where the need to keep taking them is a compulsion — is fairly common. Clinicians report that youthful solvent abusers are among their most difficult clients to cure and a great many return to abusing the drugs.

Physical dependence occurs when the body has adapted to the presence of inhalants and withdrawal symptoms occur if their use is stopped abruptly. Some chronic users, although by no means all, suffer chills, hallucinations, headaches, abdominal pains, or delirium tremens (DTs — the "shakes"). More often, however, solvent intoxication is followed by a brief period of excitement characterized by irritability, agitation, and increased heart rate.

Inhalants and Pregnancy

Little is known about the effects of inhalants on pregnancy and growth of the fetus, although preliminary animal evidence suggests that prenatal exposure to certain solvents may increase the risk of birth defects.

Who Uses Inhalants?

Solvent sniffing is frequently a group activity, with each person usually inhaling from his or her own bag or saturated cloth until intoxicated. Most commonly, users are young — between 8 and 16 years old — although some heavy users are in their late teens or older.

In a 1989 Addiction Research Foundation survey of Ontario students in grades 7 to 13, 1.9% admitted sniffing glue and 3.1% said they had used other solvents at least once in the preceding year. Among 12- and 13-year-olds, the rate of use was highest, at 2.2% for glue and 4.7% for other solvents.

The large majority of young people who abuse solvents do so only on an occasional or experimental basis. Those who regularly abuse them are more likely to: come from economically disadvantaged homes; perform less well in school and be frequently absent; and come from either unstable or broken homes, often with at least one alcoholic parent.

Inhalants and the Law

The possession or use of solvents and aerosols is not prohibited under either federal or Ontario law, and there are few drugs of abuse as cheap and as easily available. Given their many legitimate household and industrial uses, it is difficult to strictly control them. Alberta and some states in the United States have restricted the sale of glue and made it illegal to sniff solvents. Some manufacturers and retailers voluntarily limit access to these products, and community action to reduce their availability and provide other pastimes for young abusers has been recommended.

Source: Addiction Research Foundation (1991).

OPIATES

Synopsis

The opioids include both natural opiates — that is, drugs from the opium poppy — and opiate-related synthetic drugs, such as meperidine and methadone.

The opiates are found in a gummy substance extracted from the seed pod of the Asian poppy, Papaver somniferum. Opium is produced from this substance, and codeine and morphine are derived from opium. Other drugs, such as heroin, are processed from morphine or codeine.

Opiates have been used both medically and non-medically for centuries. A tincture of opium called laudanum has been widely used since the 16th century as a remedy for "nerves" or to stop coughing and diarrhea.

By the early 19th century, morphine had been extracted in a pure form suitable for solution. With the introduction of the hypodermic needle in the mid-19th century, injection of the solution became the common method of administration.

Heroin (diacetylmorphine) was introduced in 1898 and was heralded as a remedy for morphine addiction. Although heroin proved to be a more potent painkiller (analgesic) and cough suppressant than morphine, it was also more likely to produce dependence.

Of the 20 alkaloids contained in opium, only codeine and morphine are still in widespread clinical use today. In this century, many synthetic drugs have been developed with essentially the same effects as the natural opium alkaloids.

Opiate-related synthetic drugs, such as meperidine (Demerol) and methadone, were first developed to provide an analgesic that would not produce drug dependence. Unfortunately, all opioids (including naturally occurring opiate derivatives and synthetic opiate-related drugs), while effective as analgesics, can also produce dependence. (Note that where a drug name is capitalized, it is a registered trade name of the manufacturer.)

Modern research has led, however, to the development of other families of drugs. The narcotic antagonists (e.g., naloxone hydrochloride) — one of these groups — are used not as painkillers but to reverse the effects of opiate overdose.

Another group of drugs possesses both morphine-like and naloxone-like properties (e.g., pentazocine, or Talwin) and are sometimes used for pain relief because they are less likely to be abused and to cause addiction. Nevertheless, abuse of pentazocine in combination with the antihistamine tripelennamine (Pyribenzamine) was widely reported in the 1980s, particularly in several large cities in the United States. This combination became known on the street as "Ts and blues." The reformulation of Talwin, however, with the narcotic antagonist naloxone has reportedly reduced the incidence of Ts and blues use.

Appearance

Opium appears either as dark brown chunks or in powder form, and is generally eaten or smoked. Heroin usually appears as a white or brownish powder, which is dissolved in water for injection. Most street preparations of heroin contain only a small percentage of the drug, as they are diluted with sugar, quinine, or other drugs and substances. Other opiate analgesics appear in a variety of forms, such as capsules, tablets, syrups, elixirs, solutions, and suppositories. Street users usually inject opiate solutions under the skin ("skin popping") or directly into a vein or muscle, but the drugs may also be "snorted" into the nose or taken orally or rectally.

Effects
The effects of any drug depend on several factors:
- the amount taken at one time
- the user's past drug experience
- the manner in which the drug is taken
- the circumstances under which the drug is taken (the place, the user's psychological and emotional stability, the presence of other people, simultaneous use of alcohol or other drugs, etc.).

Short-term effects appear soon after a single dose and disappear in a few hours or days. Opioids briefly stimulate the higher centres of the brain but then depress activity of the central nervous system. Immediately after injection of an opioid into a vein, the user feels a surge of pleasure or a "rush." This gives way to a state of gratification; hunger, pain, and sexual urges rarely intrude.

The dose required to produce this effect may at first cause restlessness, nausea, and vomiting. With moderately high doses, however, the body feels warm, the extremities heavy, and the mouth dry. Soon, the user goes "on the nod," an alternately wakeful and drowsy state during which the world is forgotten.

As the dose is increased, breathing becomes gradually slower. With very large doses, the user cannot be roused; the pupils contract to pinpoints; the skin is cold, moist, and bluish; and profound respiratory depression resulting in death may occur. Overdose is a particular risk on the street, where the amount of drug contained in a "hit" cannot be accurately gauged.

In a treatment setting, the effects of a usual dose of morphine last three to four hours. Although pain may still be felt, the reaction to it is reduced, and the patient feels content because of the emotional detachment induced by the drug.

Long-term effects appear after repeated use over a long period. Chronic opiate users may develop endocarditis, an infection of the heart lining and valves as a result of unsterile injection techniques.

206.

Drug users who share needles are also at a high risk of acquiring AIDS (acquired immune deficiency syndrome) and HIV infection (human immunodeficiency virus). Unsterile injection techniques can also cause abscesses, cellulitis, liver disease, and even brain damage. Among users with a long history of subcutaneous injection, tetanus is common. Pulmonary complications, including various types of pneumonia, may also result from the unhealthy lifestyle of the user, as well as from the depressant effect of opiates on respiration.

Tolerance and Dependence

With regular use, tolerance develops to many of the desired effects of the opioids. This means the user must use more of the drug to achieve the same intensity of effect.

Chronic users may also become psychologically and physically dependent on opioids.

Psychological dependence exists when a drug is so central to a person's thoughts, emotions, and activities that the need to continue its use becomes a craving or compulsion.

With *physical dependence*, the body has adapted to the presence of the drug, and withdrawal symptoms occur if use of the drug is reduced or stopped abruptly. Some users take heroin on an occasional basis, thus avoiding physical dependence.

Withdrawal from opioids, which in regular users may occur as early as a few hours after the last administration, produces uneasiness, yawning, tears, diarrhea, abdominal cramps, goose bumps, and runny nose. These symptoms are accompanied by a craving for the drug.

Major withdrawal symptoms peak between 48 and 72 hours after the last dose and subside after a week. Some bodily functions, however, do not return to normal levels for as long as six months. Sudden withdrawal by heavily dependent users who are in poor health has occasionally been fatal. Opioid withdrawal, however, is much less dangerous to life than alcohol and barbiturate withdrawal

Opioids and Pregnancy

Opioid-dependent women are likely to experience complications during pregnancy and childbirth. Among their most common medical problems are anemia, cardiac disease, diabetes, pneumonia, and hepatitis. They also have an abnormally high rate of spontaneous abortion, breech delivery, caesarian section, and premature birth. Opioid withdrawal has also been linked to a high incidence of stillbirths.

Infants born to heroin-dependent mothers are smaller than average and frequently show evidence of acute infection. Most exhibit withdrawal symptoms of varying degrees and duration. The mortality rate among these infants is higher than normal.

Who Uses Opioids?

Opiates and their synthetic counterparts are used in modern medicine to relieve acute pain suffered as a result of disease, surgery, or injury; in the treatment of some forms of acute heart failure; and in the control of moderate to severe coughs or diarrhea. They are not the desired treatment for the relief of chronic pain, because their long-term and repeated use can result in drug dependence and side effects (such as constipation and mood swings). They are, however, of particular value in control of pain in the later stages of terminal illness, where the possibility of dependence is not a significant issue.

A small proportion of people for whom opioids have been medically prescribed become dependent; they are referred to as "medical addicts." Even use of non-prescription codeine products, if continued inappropriately, may get out of control. Medical advice should be sought, since withdrawal symptoms may result from abrupt cessation of use after physical dependence has been established. Because members of the medical and allied health professions have ready access to opioids, some become dependent.

The largest proportion of non-medical use, however, falls into the street-use category. Currently, heroin is the most popular opiate among street users; these users are also prone to heavy use of other psychoactive drugs, such as cocaine, alcohol, certain sedative/hypnotics, and tranquillizers.

During the past few years, synthetic opioids such as hydrocodone, hydromorphone, oxycodone, and meperidine have gained prominence as drugs of dependence. Users sometimes urge physicians to write them prescriptions for the opioid of preference. These opioids are also frequently stolen from pharmacies and sold on the street. Today, illicit use of such opioid-based medicines as Percodan, Dilaudid, and Novahistex is common.

Opioids and the Law

The federal *Narcotic Control Act* regulates the possession and distribution of all opioids. The act permits individual physicians, dentists, pharmacists, and veterinarians, as well as hospitals, to keep supplies of certain opioids. Members of the general public must obtain these drugs from such authorized sources.

Although the Act also permits the prescribing of methadone in the treatment of opioid dependence, permission is given only to specially licensed physicians, and use is governed by specific guidelines.

If tried by summary conviction, a first offence for opioid possession carries a maximum penalty of a $1,000 fine and six months imprisonment. For subsequent offences, the maximum penalty is a $2,000 fine and 12 months imprisonment. If tried by indictment, opioid possession carries a maximum penalty of seven years imprisonment.

Importing, exporting, trafficking, and possession for the purposes of trafficking are all indictable offences and carry a maximum penalty of life imprisonment. Cultivation of opium is also an indictable offence and carries a maximum penalty of seven years imprisonment.

It is illegal to obtain a prescription for opioids or any other "narcotic" from health care professionals without notifying them that you have obtained a similar prescription through another practitioner within the preceding 30 days.

Source: Addiction Research Foundation (1991).

TOBACCO

Drug Class: Central Nervous System Stimulant

Synopsis

Today, tobacco use is considered Canada's greatest public health problem. Although the percentage of cigarette smokers is steadily declining, about 6 million Canadians still smoke. Each year, at least

209.

35,000 of them die early because of their smoking. That is more each year than all the combined deaths caused by drug abuse, AIDS, murder, suicide, and motor vehicle traffic accidents. Of Canadians aged 15 years and more, 28% smoke regularly (31% of men and 26% of women). Canadian smokers use 20-25 cigarettes a day, putting them among the world's heaviest smokers.

Tobacco Smoke Components

Tobacco smoke is made up of thousands of components, the main ones being nicotine, tar, and carbon monoxide. Nicotine is the addictive agent in tobacco, tar can cause cancers and bronchial disorders, and carbon monoxide contributes to heart disease.

Nicotine is a powerful mood-altering substance that reaches the brain quickly when you smoke a cigarette.

Nicotine is also extremely toxic. A dose of about 30 mg can be fatal. Although an average Canadian cigarette contains 15-20 mg of nicotine, only a fraction is absorbed by the smoker. Canadian manufacturers report that nicotine yields in cigarettes (tested on a standard smoking machine) range from less than 0.1 mg to 1.2 mg per cigarette. For the most part, differences in the construction of the cigarette and the efficiency of the filter are responsible for this variation.

However, smokers can control the intake of nicotine considerably by adjusting their smoking technique. Long, deep inhalations, more puffs per cigarette, smoking down to the butt, or blocking the filter airflow of an ultra-low-tar brand can increase the nicotine yield to a level far above the published figure.

Tar is not a single ingredient; it is a dark sticky combination of hundreds of chemicals including poisons and cancer-causing substances. Standard tar yields of Canadian cigarettes vary from less than 1 mg to 18 mg per cigarette. As with nicotine, the tar yield of a cigarette can be higher depending on how a cigarette is smoked.

Carbon monoxide (CO), the poisonous emission from automobile engines, is also formed when tobacco is burned. CO, in smoke replaces the oxygen in red blood cells, forming carboxyhemoglobin (COHb). While nicotine causes the heart to work harder, COHb deprives it of the extra oxygen this work demands.

Among the chemicals in cigarette smoke are acids, glycerol, glycol, alcohols, aldehydes, ketones, aliphatic and aromatic hydrocarbons, phenols, and such corrosive gases as hydrogen cyanide and nitrogen oxide, as well as a heavy dose of carbon monoxide. Heart and circulatory disease, lung and other cancers, and emphysema and chronic bronchitis have been linked to some of these substances.

Effects

Short-term effects of smoking include a significant increase in heart rate and a drop in skin temperature. Respiration rate is also increased. In novice smokers, diarrhea and vomiting may occur. Although the central nervous system is, in fact, stimulated by smoking, smokers usually feel it relaxes them.

Long-term effects are mainly on the bronchopulmonary and cardiovascular systems. Smoking is the main cause of lung cancer (related to 90% of all lung cancer cases). Other factors — notably industrial carcinogens (e.g., asbestos) — may be involved, especially among smokers. An average smoker is 10 times more likely to get lung cancer than a non-smoker.

Smoking is estimated to be responsible for 30% of all cancer deaths. It is also associated with cancers of the mouth, throat, colon, pancreas, bladder, kidneys, stomach, and cervix, and related to 75% of chronic bronchitis cases and 80% of emphysema cases.

Tobacco also affects the digestive system — gastric and duodenal ulcers are twice as common and twice as likely to cause death in smokers as in non-smokers. Skin wounds may heal less quickly in smokers, partly because smoking depletes the body of vitamin C. Smokers may also have less effective immune systems than non-smokers.

Tobacco use is associated with 25% to 30% of all cardiovascular disease. Smokers have a 70% higher rate of coronary heart disease than non-smokers (it is the major smoking-related cause of death), nearly twice the risk of heart attack, and five times the risk of stroke.

The damaging effects of smoking are often increased by other factors: for example, the heavy use of such other drugs as alcohol with tobacco increases the risk of both tobacco-related cancer and other diseases of the heart and blood vessels.

Women and Tobacco

Tobacco use during pregnancy increases the risk of such complications as stillbirths, low birth weights, premature delivery, miscarriage, and Sudden Infant Death Syndrome. Women who smoke may also experience reduced fertility, increased menstrual disorders, earlier onset of menopause, and an increased risk of cervical cancer.

Women who smoke and use birth control pills are especially vulnerable, particularly after age 30. They are 39 times more likely to suffer from stroke than non-smokers who do not use the pill, and are at higher risk of contacting other circulatory diseases as well.

Nicotine and Addiction

Tobacco use can lead to physical and psychological dependence on nicotine, particularly in cigarette smokers. The United States Surgeon General's 1988 report states that "cigarettes and other forms of tobacco are just as addicting as heroin and cocaine...."

People who are physically dependent on tobacco suffer a withdrawal reaction when they stop using it. Some signs of withdrawal are: irritability, anxiety, headaches, sleep disturbances (insomnia or drowsiness), difficulty concentrating, decreased heart rate and increased appetite, and a craving for nicotine. These symptoms can last from several days to several weeks. However, desire for a cigarette and relapse to smoking can occur months after quitting, indicating that, as with other drug use, factors in addition to physical dependence play a role in nicotine addiction. Environmental events or emotional states may become conditioned signals for cigarette use.

Quitting Smoking

Although the majority of smokers want to reduce or stop smoking, attempts to do so often fail. The U.S. Surgeon General's 1988 report states that "...at least 60% of tobacco smokers have tried to quit at some time in their lives." Quitting is possible, however: the majority of people who have ever smoked give up cigarettes later in life. Although about 20% of would-be quitters stop on their first attempt, most people "give up" several times before finally stopping for good.

People who quit generally achieve the same health levels as non-smokers after a few years, especially if they stop while they are young. Risk of heart disease drops immediately; risk of lung cancer declines more gradually. Some lung disease may not be completely reversible, but even older lifetime smokers can benefit significantly from quitting.

There is no simple "cure" for smoking. It helps to find a personal reason. Cutting down or switching to ultra-low-yield brands instead of quitting may reduce exposure to smoke products, but many people just change the way they smoke — they take more or longer puffs — to get the same effect. Withdrawal symptoms subside more quickly for smokers who quit all at once than for those who gradually cut down.

Most quitters stop on their own — sometimes with the help of books, pamphlets, guides, or videos. Some prefer group support or professional counselling from a doctor, a smoking clinic, or a local health agency. No single method works for everyone; several different approaches may have to be tried.

Nicorette, a prescription gum containing nicotine, has helped some people deal with withdrawal symptoms, particularly those who are very dependent on nicotine. Other non-prescription anti-smoking products have not been shown scientifically to be effective.

Many smokers worry about weight gain if they stop smoking. Studies show that many of those who quit gain weight, but the gain is usually only a few kilograms, and can be minimized by exercising and eating low-fat foods.

Who Smokes?

Although males were once far more likely to smoke than females, smoking rates have become more similar for sexes in recent years. Between 1966 and 1986, male smoking fell from 54% to 31%. Starting from a lower peak, female smoking declined more slowly, from 32% to 26% over the same period. Today, about 28% of Canadians over the age of 15 smoke cigarettes. Teenagers are much less likely to smoke than adults.

People are more likely to smoke if their parents, family, and friends do. Those who drop out of high school are more likely to smoke than those with more education. Smoking is also related to occupation. Fewer managers and professionals smoke than do people in other white-collar occupations. Daily cigarette use is most prevalent among blue-collar workers and the unemployed.

Tobacco and the Law

In Canada, the purchase or possession of tobacco by anyone under 16 years of age is a federal criminal offence under the *Tobacco Restraint*

Act. The maximum penalty for a first offence is a reprimand and the maximum for a second offence is a $1 fine. It is also a federal criminal offence to sell or supply tobacco products to anyone under the age of 16.

In 1988, Parliament passed two tobacco acts. One dramatically limited tobacco advertising and the other severely restricted smoking in federal workplaces and transportation facilities. Ontario has also enacted legislation that limits smoking to designated areas. In Ontario, the *Minors' Protection Act* makes it a provincial offence to sell or supply tobacco in any form to a person under 18 years (except where minors are on errands for their parents or guardians and have a written request). The maximum penalty for this offence is $500. A maximum fine of $25,000 applies to corporations.

Public Smoking

Evidence indicates that exposure to a smoke-filled environment can affect healthy non-smokers. As a result, some municipalities have introduced non-smoking bylaws in public places. Evidence suggests exposure to environmental tobacco smoke increases the risk of lung cancer in otherwise healthy non-smokers. "Passive smoking" may also cause heart disease.

Second-hand smoke is hazardous to people with allergies, those with heart or lung disease, and children. Infants of parents who smoke at home have twice the rate of ear infections, coughs, colds, pneumonias, and bronchitis in their first year.

Source: Addiction Research Foundation (1991).

If You Want More Information

NATIONAL ORGANIZATIONS

Canadian Centre on Substance Abuse (CCSA)   www.ccsa.ca
75 Albert Street, Suite 300
Ottawa, ON K1P 5E7   Tel: (613) 235-4048

  Fetal Alcohol Syndrome (FAS)
   Information Service   Toll Free: 1-800-559-4514
                                        Fax: (613) 235-8101

*Promotes debate on substance use issues and encourages public
participation in reducing the harm associated with drug use.
Supports and assists organizations involved in substance use
treatment, prevention and educational programming.*

National Clearinghouse on Substance Abuse
75 Albert Street, Suite 300
Ottawa, ON K1P 5E7

  Publications   Tel: (613) 235-4048

*Collects and disseminates information on substance use, nationally
and internationally.*

Canadian Council for Tobacco Control   www.cctc.ca
(Formerly Canadian Council on Smoking and Health)
75 Albert Street, Suite 508
Ottawa, ON K1P 5E7   Tel: (613) 567-3050
                              Toll Free: 1-800-267-5234
                                        Fax: (613) 567-2730

Collects and disseminates information on smoking.

215.

PROVINCIAL ORGANIZATIONS

NEWFOUNDLAND

Addictions Services
Provincial Office
1st Floor, West Block, Confederation Building
P.O. Box 8700
St. John's, NF A1B 4J6

Tel: (709) 729-0623
Fax: (709) 729-5824

NOVA SCOTIA

Drug Dependency Services
P.O. Box 896
Dartmouth, NS B2Y 3Z6

Tel: (902) 368-4120
Fax: (902) 368-6229

PRINCE EDWARD ISLAND

P.E.I. Addiction Services
Mount Herbert
P.O. Box 2000
PEI C1A 7N8

Tel: (902) 368-4120
Fax: (902) 368-6229

NEW BRUNSWICK

Department of Health & Community Services
Carleton Place, P.O. Box 5100
520 King Street
Fredericton, NB E3B 5G8

Tel: (506) 457-4983
Fax: (506) 453-2726

  Library

Tel: (506) 453-3715

QUÉBEC

L'Association des intervenants en toxicomanie du Québec Inc.
505 St. Helene Street, 2nd Floor
Longueuil, QC J4K 3R5

Tel: (450) 646-3271
Fax: (450) 646-3275

216.

Centre québecois de documentation en toxicomanie
950 De Louvain East Street   Tel: (514) 385-3490
Montreal, QC H2M 2E8   Fax: (514) 385-5778

Comité permanent de lutte à la toxicomanie
950 De Louvain East Street   Tel: (514) 389-6336
Montreal, QC H2M 2E8   Fax: (514) 389-1830

ONTARIO

Centre for Addiction and Mental Health
33 Russell Street
Toronto, ON M5S 2S1   Tel: 1-800-463-6273
  Library   Tel: (416) 595-6144
                              Fax: (416) 595-6036

  Drug and Alcohol
  Registry of Treatment (DART) Tel: 1-800-565-8603

Ministry of Health
Communication and Information
9th Floor, Hepburn Block, 80 Grosvenor St.
Toronto, ON M7A 1S2   Tel: (416) 327-4343

Women's Health Council Secretariat
(Formerly Women's Health Bureau)
880 Bay Street   Tel: (416) 327-8348
Toronto, ON M7A 1R3   Fax: (416) 327-3200

MANITOBA

Addictions Foundation of Manitoba
1031 Portage Avenue   Tel: (204) 944-6200
Winnipeg, MN R3G 0R8   Fax: (204) 786-7768
  Library   Tel: (204) 944-6233
                              Fax: (204) 774-8091

  Women's and Family Services
  586 River Avenue   Tel: (204) 944-6229
  Winnipeg, MN R3L 0E8   Fax: (204) 284-5520

SASKATCHEWAN

Saskatchewan Mental Health Programs Branch

1810 Albert Street	Resource Centre:	Tel:	(306) 525-9543
Regina, SK S4P 2S8		Fax:	(306) 525-9579

ALBERTA

Alberta Alcohol & Drug Abuse Commission (AADAC)

10909 Jasper Avenue, 2nd Floor	Tel:	(403) 427-7319
Edmonton, AB T5J 4M9	Toll Free:	1-800-280-9616

BRITISH COLUMBIA

Alcohol & Drug Services

Adult Clinical and Addiction Services Branch
Ministry of Health & Ministry Responsible for Seniors

1810 Blanchard Street, 3rd Floor	Tel:	(604) 953-3113
Victoria, BC VAT 4J1	Fax:	(604) 953-3044
Alcohol & Drug Information Service	Tel:	(604) 660-9382

**B.C. Prevention
Resource Centre**

	(BC only)	Toll Free:	1-800-663-1880
Suite 2730 Commercial Drive		Tel:	(604) 874-8452
Vancouver, BC V5N 5P4		Fax:	(604) 874-9348

YUKON

Alcohol & Drug Services

P.O. Box 2703 (H7)		
Whitehorse, YK Y1A 2C6	Tel:	(867) 667-5777

NORTHWEST TERRITORIES

Department of Health & Social Services   Tel: (867) 873-7737

Community Health Programs

Government of Northwest Territories

P.O. Box 1320	Tel:	(867) 873-7738
Yellowknife, NT X1A 2L9	Fax:	(867) 873-7706

218.

OTHER RESOURCES

Contact the Centre for Addiction and Mental Health's 24-hour information line (1-800-463-6273) to obtain lists of resources (books, manuals, videos) on women and substance use.

You can contact your provincial government for a listing or resources and other organizations that may be more relevant to you.